FOR THE
WIN

KEVIN WERBACH AND DAN HUNTER

FOR THE
WIN

The Power of

GAMIFICATION

and Game Thinking in Business,
Education, Government, and Social Impact

REVISED AND UPDATED EDITION

WHARTON
SCHOOL
PRESS
Philadelphia

© 2020, 2012 by Kevin Werbach and Dan Hunter

Published by Wharton School Press
The Wharton School
University of Pennsylvania
3620 Locust Walk
300 Steinberg Hall-Dietrich Hall
Philadelphia, PA 19104
Email: whartonschoolpress@wharton.upenn.edu
Website: wsp.wharton.upenn.edu

Ebook ISBN: 978-1-61363-104-1
Paperback ISBN: 978-1-61363-105-8

For Nate and Elena—DH
For Eli and Esther—KW

Contents

Introduction
Why Can't Life Be Fun?

Each year in the United States alone, almost 800,000 people suffer strokes, according to the Centers for Disease Control and Prevention. For hundreds of thousands of people fortunate to survive, the road to recovery is long, cumbersome, and at times demotivating.

A South Korean–headquartered company, Neofect, is aiming to change that. One of its products is the Rapael Smart Glove. It prompts patients to move their fingers, hands, and wrists, with a twist. They're not just moving their fingers—on the screen, they're playing catch, fishing, or refilling their wine glasses. Over time, patients progress to different difficulty levels in their rehabilitation process.

It's not a video game, exactly. No company would market a game that involves, say, chopping food, and nothing else. *Boring.* Yet even such dull repetition can feel motivating and fun (sort of) when the feedback, rewards, and structure of the experience are designed right. And that's a big deal when the point isn't to sell games but to rehabilitate patients.

This is a classic example of the now-established practice of gamification. In this case, at least one study has found significant benefit pairing game-assisted therapies with more conventional methods. In addition to the smart glove, Neofect has developed a smart board, a pegboard, and more.

For thousands of years, we've created things called games that tap the tremendous psychic power of fun. A well-designed game is a guided missile to the motivational heart of the human psyche. Applying the lessons that games can teach could change your business, the way you learn or teach, even your life. The premise of this book is that fun is an extraordinarily valuable tool to address serious pursuits like marketing, productivity enhancement, education, innovation, customer engagement, human resources, and sustainability. We are not talking about fleeting enjoyment—rather, the deep fun that comes from extended interaction with well-designed games.

It turns out that games can be used in a wide range of settings. Consider the following set of scenarios: A management consultant walks into her supervisor's office to announce she's jumping ship to a competitor. Sure, the firm paid her a hefty salary for the past five years, but one consulting firm is the same as another, right?

A student struggles to pay attention to the assignment for tomorrow's class. He knows the grade is important, but the material just seems pointless. He does the work, but only because he has to, not because he cares about what he's studying.

A mother wheels her shopping cart through the supermarket aisles, as her toddler becomes unruly in the child seat. She grabs products from the shelves, usually picking the familiar brands without much thought.

Disengaged, demotivated, disempowered, and disconnected. Isn't that how employees, students, and customers always are—and always will be?

Now imagine a different world. The consultant basks in the status boost when her team tops the firm's internal leaderboard. The student feels rewarded—mentally and by his instructor—when he reaches the next level and unlocks new material. And the harried mother feels a jolt of pure joy when she earns a coveted badge for buying the ingredients for a nutritious meal (and realizes it costs less than that packaged junk she bought before).

By at least some measures, the people in the first vignettes are doing their jobs effectively. Perhaps we want our leaders to be ruthless, our students to mechanically complete their work, and our consumers to be buying unthinkingly. But an exclusive focus on short-term factors will produce short-term benefits at best, while risking much larger long-term costs. These individuals are not engaged: They are phoning it in. It's hard to imagine them or any of the organizations they interact with producing the next great innovation, viral hit product, or visionary CEO. And no one seems to be having much fun. But what's fun got to do with business (or life), anyway?

A lot.

Gamification can change lives for the better. We've told you a bit about Neofect. We'll introduce you to SuperBetter, which demonstrated significant results treating depression, concussion symptoms, and the mental health harms of the COVID-19 pandemic through game thinking. You're almost certainly already aware of fitness tracking systems that encourage users to get up and walk thousands of steps, motivated by a simple buzz on their wrists or the digital badge when they hit their target. Many thousands of newly healthy people can attest to the fact that games make a difference.

At the other end of the spectrum, the ride-hailing giant Uber once used gamification to persuade its drivers to work longer hours than they otherwise wanted to. Influenced by the same kinds of techniques used in video games, drivers were psychologically manipulated to work harder, to meet goals that were in the interests of the company, not those of the drivers. The backlash, when it came, was fierce. Later in this book we'll show how similarly serious ethical issues—together with public relations disasters—have arisen as a result of the gamification efforts of Disney, various governments, and the fintech start-up Robinhood.

The story of gamification isn't fun and games by any means. It's really serious. When used carefully and thoughtfully, gamification produces great outcomes for users, in ways that are hard to replicate through other methods. Other times, companies misuse the "guided missile" of gamification to have people work and do things in ways that are against their self-interest, and are clearly worrying. Gamification has even been implicated in suicide.

In the remainder of this book, we will take you through research and examples to show you how, why, and when gamification works, and guide you in developing these methods for your purposes. And just as importantly, we'll show you what not to do with gamification.

Games and Gamification

In 2012, when the first edition of this book appeared, making the real world more game-like still sounded far-fetched. Then on July 6, 2016, a tiny subsidiary of Google released an augmented reality mobile game. By the end of the year, Pokémon Go was downloaded half a billion times. By 2018, it had 150 million monthly active users worldwide. Pokémon Go turned millions of ordinary people walking around their neighborhoods into hunters and trainers of tiny monsters, which magically appeared on their smartphone screens. Pokémon Go isn't gamification—it's an actual *game*—but it highlights how technology can fuse game-like experiences with quotidian reality. What if those same techniques were applied to other purposes?

To really understand why gamification works, think about a time when you were engrossed in a game. For some of you it may have been golf; for others, chess or Scrabble; for those who like video games, it may have been Fortnite or Minecraft. Wouldn't you like to feel that same sense of accomplishment and flow in your work—or to feel engaged and rewarded by your consumer interactions with companies? Organizations whose employees, communities, and customers are deeply engaged will outperform those that cannot engender authentic motivation. This is especially true in a world where competition is global and technology has radically lowered barriers to entry. Engagement is your competitive advantage. Game-design techniques provide your means to achieve it.

Games have been around since the beginning of human civilization. Today, video games make up a massive global industry that generates nearly $150 billion per year. Hundreds of millions of people in every corner of the globe spend hundreds of billions of minutes every month playing console, PC, online, and mobile games. Games are popular in every demographic, gender, and age group, but they are especially pervasive among those more recently entering the workforce.

Our starting question is this: What if you could reverse-engineer what makes games effective and graft it into a business environment, a learning setting, or some other serious context? That's the premise of the practice called *gamification*. Our goal is to show you exactly how gamification can be used as a powerful asset for your organization.

One point to make clear at the outset: This isn't a book about video games. It's not about the games industry, the gamer generation, the societal impact (good or bad) of game playing, or how much the latest release of Call of Duty cost to produce. It's not about 3-D virtual worlds, advergames, or edutainment. It's not even about the internet or digital business. Sure, we'll talk about such things, but only as context. This is a book about how you can use gamification to improve your business practices. And when we say "business" in this book, it's really a shorthand for any serious motivational context. It could be a teacher looking to motivate students in a class, a runner pushing themselves to keep going, a community trying to cut its electricity usage, or even analysts at a secret US military facility scanning phone and email records for terrorist conversations. (Yes, they gamified their approach too.)

Gamification does not mean turning all business into a game, any more than innovation turns it into an R&D lab or Six Sigma turns it into a factory production line. Gamification is a powerful toolkit to apply to your existing challenges, whatever their nature. Many of the best examples of game mechanics in business, education, and other contexts don't even look like games to those involved. The essence of games isn't entertainment. It's a fusion of human nature and skillful design. Those hundreds of millions of video game players spend all those hours because the games were rigorously and skillfully designed, based on decades of real-world experience and an understanding of human psychology.

Knowing how to conduct a market segmentation or a minimum viable product analysis won't show you how to create enduringly engaging experiences. That's why most business managers find gamification so new and challenging. The reverse, however, is equally true. Expertise in game programming, level design, art direction, or playtesting won't help you calculate the lifetime value of a customer, manage a team, develop a corporate training program, or choose the right business strategy. In our research with companies and in teaching the world's first course on the business practice of gamification at Wharton, we've seen both the confusion and the insights that emerge when business practices and game design meet.

Underlying our effort is the recognition that traditional incentive structures often fall short. The carrot and the stick don't cut it anymore; and money, status, and the threat of punishment only work up to a point. In a world of near-infinite choices, the old techniques are rapidly becoming less effective. Economists have been forced to acknowledge that people sometimes act in predictably irrational ways that frustrate basic tenets of management and marketing. How can firms use this knowledge to positive effect?

Research into human motivation gathered from scholarly literature demonstrates that people will feel motivated by well-designed game features. Monetary rewards aren't even necessary, because *the game itself is the reward*. Video game players will, for example, invest enormous resources into acquiring virtual objects and achievements that have no tangible value. The blockbuster Fortnite alone made $2.4 billion that way in 2018, according to Nielsen's SuperData Research division, *even though it's completely free to play*.

Based on numbers such as these, an industry now trumpets the virtues of gamification. We're encouraged by this development, but we also want to sound a note of caution. It's easy to focus on the surface attributes of games and miss the deeper aspects. If gamification is just a gloss on existing marketing or management practices, or traditional rewards in shiny packages, it won't produce any added value. It could well make things worse. There's a reason most video games fail: Game design is hard.

Whether you're an executive at a large corporation considering a gamification project, a staffer at a nonprofit seeking new ways to make a difference in your community, a student trying to understand the skills you'll need for job opportunities in a burgeoning field, or anything in between, our goal is to provide you with a pragmatic guidebook that includes all the basics you will need to begin experimenting with gamification in your organization. Throughout, we attempt to provide you with a sophisticated understanding of the concepts around gamification, and we provide frameworks and step-by-step instructions to implement your ideas. Drawing on our research and conversations with executives, activists, and leaders, we reveal in *For the Win* how organizations of all types are putting gamification into practice. There are also numerous concepts drawn from academic scholarship in management, marketing, industrial organization, psychology, and other business fields. (Key references are provided at the end of the book for those interested in going deeper.) As the faddish aspects of gamification have faded away, these well-grounded insights remain valuable.

In emphasizing the practical focus of this book, we don't mean to give short shrift to the deeper implications of the techniques we describe. Gamification done right points toward a radical transformation in the conduct of business. If fun matters, it's because people matter. People matter as autonomous agents striving for fulfillment, not as black boxes or simplistic rational profit maximizers. Even as more of life is mediated through remote networked software systems executing programmed algorithms—in fact, because of it—the mysterious factors that make life meaningful should be a central concern of leaders. Recognizing the power of what we call "game thinking" is one step on that path.

Why We Wrote This Book

In the first edition of this book, we told the story of how our interest in gamification grew out of the experience of playing together in the multiplayer online game World of Warcraft. We'd spend our nights killing virtual monsters and chatting with our guildmates, most of whom were academic games scholars or professional video game designers. Then we'd spend our days teaching about the radical promise of the internet in business schools and universities. We began to think about the arbitrary points-based system that we call grades, and the other aspects of course design to motivate and assess students. There's nothing derogatory in the observation that education and work are really just games. So, if that's true, we began to ask ourselves, why not make them better games?

We started to research gamification, and at Wharton we co-taught the first-ever business school course on the topic. We found that although there were great books on game design and on the speculative implications of games for society, there was nothing in print that gave a clear and rigorous explanation of how and why to build gamified systems. We realized there was a real need for a research-grounded yet pragmatic guide that explained how to do gamification properly. We wrote the initial edition of this book as the first how-to and why-to for gamification.

The book struck a nerve with both practitioners and researchers and quickly became the standard text defining the principles and practices of gamification. *For the Win* has been translated into seven languages and cited in more than 2,000 subsequent works. We published a short companion volume, *The Gamification Toolkit*, which elaborates on the functions of all the game elements and goes into detail on some valuable success cases.

Since the first edition was released, Kevin created a massive open online course (MOOC) about gamification that has enrolled more than half a million people around the world, and Dan launched several start-ups that employ gamification techniques. And, of course, we continued to play games in online worlds—it's just that these days we run around killing dragons with our kids.

Two things have changed dramatically since 2012: the sheer number of real-world gamification examples and the volume of academic papers investigating these techniques. This new edition thoroughly updates the examples and incorporates the most prominent research findings throughout. In particular, the mistakes we warned about in the first edition of the book—ineffective slapdash gamification and overly effective gamification that is just abusive manipulation—went from hypotheticals to all-too-common realities. We've bulked up the sections of the book showing how to steer clear of these pitfalls. However, we've avoided making the material too dense to be useful. This isn't a textbook for school. It's your playbook for the real world.

The Big New Trends

The first edition of this book appeared just as gamification was cresting its hype wave. Google searches for the term were skyrocketing, consulting firms were predicting massive market growth, and specialized consultancies like Bunchball, Badgeville, and Gamification.co were popping up everywhere. Most have folded or pivoted. Organizations nowadays rarely feel the need to trumpet their gamification activities, because their competitors are gamifying as well. The expertise has diffused beyond the specialists as gamification becomes part of the standard business toolkit. Those are indicators of success for the technique.

The world today is different in many ways from the world when we wrote the first edition of *For the Win*. Yet games haven't lost their pull on us; they never will. We can all still use a healthy dose of fun to achieve our goals in business—and beyond. Those Google search numbers flattened out but never really dropped. At times it's frustrating to see an article describe gamification as a new concept. Don't people understand that, for an internet-based business technique, it's already middle aged, if not more mature?

In returning to this material eight years after the first edition, what surprised us most was how little the core frameworks needed to be updated. Our approach to gamification is grounded in time-tested insights from management, psychology, design, and other fields. Concepts such as engagement loops, player types, and the triad of intrinsic motivators may remain unfamiliar in mainstream business and educational contexts, but they are well established in their home disciplines. Our own experience, and that of many practitioners, has demonstrated the effectiveness of the guidance in this book.

That said, there have been some significant changes in the development of gamification since we wrote the first edition. These can be boiled down to five notable trends:

1. **Gamification has expanded well beyond the domain of business.** The subtitle for the first edition of the book was *How Game Thinking Can Revolutionize Your Business*, which now sounds much too limited. As we discuss below, game mechanics are widely dispersed and are found not only in business settings but also in health, government, philanthropy, and day-to-day life.

2. **Gamification has been incorporated into the widespread adoption of "nudges" to change people's behavior.** Named after the wildly influential book by cognitive psychologist Richard Thaler and legal academic and policy maven Cass Sunstein, nudging involves creating "choice architectures" to push people toward making better decisions—saving for retirement, eating better, or even being recruited for military service. The concept of nudging has been incredibly significant over the past decade, resulting in numerous academic articles and practical projects along with no end of government initiatives. The core psychological basis of nudging is precisely the same as we find in gamification, and in Level 3 we will explore some of the ways that nudges are used in gamification mechanics.

3. **Points, badges, and leaderboards are no longer the gold standard of gamification.** As we discuss in Level 4, these three mechanics are still a core feature of many gamification projects, but nowadays we see many more game mechanics that intelligently use different mechanics to meet their designers' ends. We will explore when and why you should use each, in the chapters below.

4. **Most of the gamification practiced today doesn't arise from a stand-alone effort to apply game design techniques.** Gamification is mostly seen as just good design practice. So, for example, having virtual fireworks explode on the screen of a health app when the user hits a meaningful goal is a powerful motivator by itself. The app designers don't necessarily need to create an elaborate game-like experience. The good news is that it's easier than ever to get started with gamification. The bad news is that if you don't appreciate *why* the fireworks are effective, and the deeper design patterns they exemplify, you won't be nearly as successful.

5. **Unprincipled and sometimes unethical gamification is on the rise.** We warned about this in the original edition, but the problem has become significantly worse. It's clear that some gamification designers have cottoned on to the fact that games can make people do things against their interest, because they fulfill a shallow need or on the surface seem "fun." This is a regrettable trend, and one that we address in even greater detail in this edition.

We will explore each of these trends and how they play out, as we dig into the specifics of gamification in the chapters that follow.

A Map of the Territory

For the Win covers the concepts required to implement gamification successfully in any kind of organization. Like many games, it progresses through a series of levels. As you master each concept, you'll be ready to take the next step.

At Level 1, you will gain a clear overview of gamification. At Level 2, we show you how to determine whether gamification will work for your specific problem. Here we teach you how to approach problems like a game designer. That means understanding exactly what a game is and the basics of game thinking. At Level 3, we get you to dig down into the motivations of the users of your gamification system and ask how gamification can better engage them. Decades of research reveal surprising facts about the best ways to motivate behavior. We take a look at specific gamification techniques at Level 4, including the hierarchy of game dynamics, mechanics, and components.

At that point you will have the basics, but then it will be time to integrate them. At Level 5, we lay out how to put gamification to work through a six-step design process. At Level 6, we examine important risks, such as legal and ethical problems, overly simplistic approaches to implementation, and what happens when your players turn the tables on you.

If you're reading this book to learn more about what gamification is and how it works, you'll have a comprehensive foundation. If you're looking to implement gamification in your organization, you will be ready to experiment on your own or with a partner or team. Gamification isn't something you can expect to get right and leave unchanged for an extended period, because your players will demand more. Our goal is to put you ahead of the game. This book has everything you need to start. Additional resources are available through Kevin's Coursera MOOC, https://www.coursera.org/learn/gamification.

Let the games begin.

A Note on the Title

"For the win," or FTW for short, is a gamer term believed to be derived from old-school TV game shows like *Hollywood Squares*, in which a player could win the game with a correct answer. It's used as an endorsement of a tool or practice that will lead to success in any context—as in "Daily exercise FTW!" We find it an appropriate moniker. Gamification is a technique that businesses can use to be more successful. We hope you will use this book to help your organization win in whatever ways you choose.

Level 1

Getting into the Game
An Introduction to Gamification

> *Everything in the future online is going to look like a*
> *multiplayer game.*
> —Former Google CEO Eric Schmidt

Congratulations! You've begun! You're at Gamification Level 1.

At this initial level, we explain why you should care about gamification, and we answer some basic questions:

- *Why are games valuable in serious business contexts?*
- *What is gamification?*
- *How can game concepts be employed in your business?*
- *When is gamification most effective?*

If we asked you to picture the most fun you can have at work, chances are that information security is not going to be what comes to mind.

Indeed, for most people, practicing good information security hygiene is about as exciting as mandatory fire drills. Sure, everyone knows it's important: Major global firms today face a huge challenge in teaching thousands of employees the best practices to avoid phishing attacks, theft of passwords, social engineering, and other hacker tricks. We all know that the consequences for companies are immense if hackers gain access to their systems: millions of dollars in damage and immeasurable reputational harms. But it is so dull.

Figure 1.1: Super Hacker Land, One of Accenture's Information Security Training Games

Surely there is a way to make this fun?

Accenture, the professional services giant with a global workforce of over 500,000, takes information security *very* seriously. So seriously, in fact, that it has turned its training programs into games. Accenture's Information Security (IS) Advocates program offers a series of game-like modules: Super Hacker Land is an island filled with cyber threats (figure 1.1); Uncovered puts employees in the role of a spy infiltrating an Accenture office; Home Safe Home illustrates the security risks when, as suddenly became more frequent during the COVID-19 pandemic, employees work from home.

The program itself functions as a kind of game. Employees can earn bronze, silver, and gold badges based on how much training they complete. As with the Microsoft Language Quality Game, there's also competition among Accenture regions.

The results have been dramatic. More than 90% of Accenture employees earned Advocate status by completing essential training modules. Advocates are 50% less likely to experience a security incident and perform 70% better on phishing tests compared with non-Advocate employees.

Making Microsoft Windows Fun

Hundreds of millions of people use Microsoft Windows and Office daily. These software systems were built by thousands of developers, modified repeatedly over a period of years, and customized for every major world language. Bugs and other errors are inevitable. Microsoft's testing group is responsible for ferreting them out.

It's a monumental task. Automated systems aren't sufficient; the only way to ensure quality is for a vast number of eyeballs to review every feature, every usage case, and every dialog box in every language. It's not just the scale of the problem: Rigorously testing software is, much of the time, mind-numbingly boring. Even for a company with the resources of Microsoft, it's no easy matter to find enough people.

If you were Ross Smith, a director in Microsoft's testing group at the time of Windows 7, you probably wouldn't think that fun was the answer. Software testing is serious business, with solemn financial and even legal implications for the company. You may be surprised to learn, then, that Smith solved the problem through games. His group pioneered the concept of software-quality games that turned the testing process into an engaging, enjoyable experience.

Smith's group recruited Microsoft employees around the world to review Windows dialog boxes for their languages in their spare time. They were awarded points for each suspicious bit of language they found and ranked on a leaderboard (a public "high score" list) based on their success (figure 1.2). To ensure players didn't just click through screens without reading them, the organizers sprinkled in deliberate errors and obvious mistranslations. The game's scoring system tracked the performance of individuals and regions.

The Language Quality Game created a competitive dynamic. Employees wanted to win, and they wanted their regions to win. The Microsoft offices in Japan topped the regional leaderboard by taking a day off from other work to weed out localization errors. All told, 4,500 participants reviewed over half a million Windows 7 dialog boxes and logged 6,700 bug reports, resulting in hundreds of significant fixes.

Figure 1.2: The Microsoft Language Quality Game for Hindi Localization

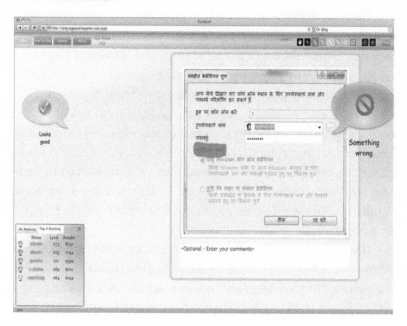

Not only did they go above and beyond their work responsibilities, but a large number of them described the process as enjoyable and even addicting. Smith's group went on to develop a series of workplace games to improve the quality of Microsoft products.

The Microsoft and Accenture initiatives are examples of a burgeoning set of business techniques that go by the name "gamification." They show how fun can be employed strategically to address virtually any serious goal. These techniques are coming soon, if they haven't already, to a business near you.

There are now over 100 gamification software services, along with many toolkits to plug into existing websites. These products capture only a fraction of gamification activity, because so many organizations—Microsoft and Accenture included—develop their own solutions in-house. Pretty much every major company we've looked at has a gamification project, or several. Hundreds of teachers and professors have gamified their classes in a variety of ways.

The technical requirements for gamification are modest, and there are lots of platforms out there to help you. It's the design principles that can be challenging, which is why they are the focus of this book.

How Gamification Solves Problems

The organizations we describe in this book have realized that the power of games extends beyond the objectives of the games themselves. A flight simulator can teach a pilot how to handle dangerous situations that may occur during landing. But if you're running an airline, you also care about whether your flight attendants exude a positive attitude, your baggage handlers do their best to get suitcases out on time, and your customers express loyalty. Gamification techniques can help organizations improve every one of these mission-critical activities.

Four non-game contexts are particularly prominent: internal, external, behavior change, and crowdsourcing (figure 1.3).

Figure 1.3: Relationship Between Gamification Categories

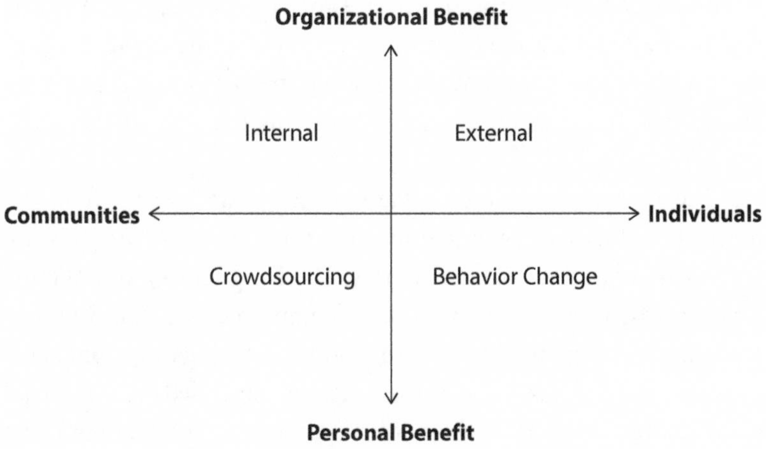

Organizational Benefit

Internal | External

Communities ← → **Individuals**

Crowdsourcing | Behavior Change

Personal Benefit

Internal Gamification

Microsoft's and Accenture's initiatives are examples of *internal gamification*. In these scenarios, companies use gamification to improve productivity within the organization in order to foster innovation, enhance camaraderie, or otherwise derive positive business results through their own community of employees. In a survey by online training firm TalentLMS, more than 80% of employees using gamified systems agreed that game elements made them more productive, happier, and more engaged at work.

Internal programs are sometimes called enterprise gamification, but you don't have to be a large enterprise. Even small companies can apply game-design techniques to enhance productivity. Gamification of learning fits within the internal category as well. We've already seen that with Accenture's training programs. The same techniques apply to schools, universities, lifelong learning, and other educational contexts.

There are two distinguishing attributes of internal gamification. First, the players are already part of a defined community. The organization knows who they are, and they interact with each other on a regular basis. They may not have shared affinities like the community of Harry Potter fans; in fact, they may be quite diverse in their perspectives and interests. However, they share reference points such as the corporate culture and desire for advancement and status within the organization. Accenture employees care about demonstrating how well they and their regions are performing, and they also have a shared commitment to protecting the firm against security breaches.

The other aspect of internal gamification flows from the first. The motivational dynamics of gamification must interact with existing management and reward structures. The Language Quality Game was effective because its players weren't employed as localization testers. They participated in what Ross Smith calls organizational citizenship behavior, not because their salaries depended on it. Internal gamification can work for core job requirements, but there must be some additional motivation. That could be the status of winning a coveted employee award or the opportunity to learn new skills.

External Gamification

External gamification involves your customers or prospective customers. These applications are generally driven by marketing objectives. Gamification here is a way to improve the relationships between businesses and customers, producing increased engagement, identification with the product, stronger loyalty, and ultimately higher revenues.

A good example is the *Record Searchlight*, a daily newspaper in Redding, California. Virtually every newspaper faces a quandary as readers shift from print to digital. The reporting, editorial, and investigative functions that newspapers provide depend on revenues from advertising and subscriptions, which largely evaporate when readers use online search engines to get their news. Management at the *Record Searchlight* realized that it could combat this trend if it built a sustainable community on its advertising-supported website. The challenge was to turn passive readers into engaged users who would spend time interacting with multiple articles on the site and recommend them to friends.

To solve this problem, the *Record Searchlight* implemented a badge system for comments on its online articles. Users were rewarded with badges for particular numbers of insightful comments, as flagged by other readers. A badge is a distinctive icon that shows up on a user's profile when he or she reaches a defined set of requirements. That may not seem terribly important, but badges can be powerful motivators. They signify achievements and display them for all to see. Think about the patches used by the Boy Scouts, the insignias on military uniforms, or the "Harvard graduate" line on a résumé. Gamified badges serve the same function digitally.

The paper's primary goal was to increase engagement with its website. After three months, the *Record Searchlight* saw a 10% rise in comment volume, and the time spent on the site increased by about

25% per session. Another goal was to improve the quality of conversations on the site. By encouraging readers to reward good comments by other readers, the badges reduced the number of offensive and problematic comments. That reduced editorial costs for the paper, and it made the online discussion area a more valuable tool for retaining readers.

As a form of marketing, external gamification can take advantage of all the sophistication of modern data-driven marketing practices. Gamification adds a richer toolkit to understand customer motivation. It's also a great way to retain and stimulate the customers you already have. The creators of the business messaging service Slack originally built it as part of a failed massively multiplayer game. They left in several endearing touches, such as the cheery Slackbot persona (what a game designer would call a "nonplayer character") that periodically reminds you about important features. Slack is all about getting work done. But that doesn't mean it can't be fun.

Behavior-Change Gamification

Behavior-change gamification seeks to form beneficial new habits among a population. That can involve anything from encouraging people to make better health choices, such as eating better or working out more, to redesigning the classroom to facilitate kids learning more while actually enjoying school, to building systems that help people save more money for retirement without lecturing them about how poor they are going to be in a few years' time. Generally, these new habits produce desirable societal outcomes: less obesity, lower medical expenses, a more effective educational system, and better financial decisions, although they can also create private benefits, such as reducing corporate healthcare expenses. A 2016 review of 19 research papers on gamification for health and well-being found predominantly positive results.

Jane McGonigal is a game designer and author. She made a name for herself creating large-scale location-based and social-impact games. Then one day she hit her head on a cabinet in her office. Weeks later, the concussion symptoms hadn't gone away, and she began feeling suicidal. To motivate herself to follow her doctor's recommended steps for recovery, she made up a game. "Jane the Concussion Slayer" would earn points for calling friends and walking outside, and lose them for drinking caffeine. It helped her stay on track.

McGonigal later formalized the idea into SuperBetter, a mobile application to help people gain resilience and address mental health challenges. SuperBetter users adopt a secret identity, complete quests, collect power-ups, and recruit allies in order to battle bad guys such as depression, anxiety, and chronic pain. As communities across the world entered into stay-at-home orders amid the COVID-19 pandemic, SuperBetter added a Stay-at-Home Scavenger Hunt, designed to increase social connection during physical distancing. For two weeks, players were challenged to find daily items within their homes and then share them through the app and social media.

While describing getting off the couch as "the battle against the Sticky Chair" may sound silly, turning a chore into part of a game can shift our mental framing. A randomized controlled trial study found SuperBetter had positive effects in treating depression, and a clinical trial at a university hospital found similar effectiveness for teenagers experiencing concussion symptoms.

Many other apps, health-care organizations, and nonprofits are using gamification techniques for everything from encouraging low-income kids to increase physical activity to helping people quit smoking to getting older people to take their medications regularly. In President Barack Obama's administration, a White House initiative led by the Office of the National Coordinator for Health Information Technology and the Office of Science and Technology Policy explored games for health as a major national program. All of these efforts have in common the recognition that motivation is at the heart of sustained behavior change, and games are among the most powerful motivational tools.

Crowdsourcing Gamification

Finally, gamification is a great way to mobilize collections of individuals to work on problems, a process known as *crowdsourcing*. Some crowdsourcing platforms, such as Amazon's Mechanical Turk, pay people for every task they complete. In other cases, no money changes hands. Gamification can provide an additional layer of motivation. Foldit, created by a University of Washington scientist, has hundreds of thousands of volunteers who help solve complex protein-folding problems from their homes. Foldit's colorful interface makes the experience feel like a puzzle-solving game, and there's the appeal of helping to advance important biomedical research.

Kaggle, a start-up acquired by Google in 2017, crowdsources data science challenges. It has run hundreds of competitions for major corporations, hedge funds, government agencies, and other organizations, with prizes sometimes in the hundreds of thousands of dollars. Kaggle's three million users have developed algorithms to predict home values, analyze medical images, improve passenger screening for the US Department of Homeland Security, and even help physicists find the elusive Higgs boson particle.

Winning the competitions is one motivation for the teams that participate, but not the only one. Kaggle users earn points, virtual medals, and expertise tiers (from contributor to master) based on their performance (figure 1.4). The platform also rewards users for high-quality posts on discussion boards, for sharing datasets, and for posting software code that others can use. This progression system changes the win-or-lose experience into an ongoing growth process. The game-like aspects make Kaggle feel like a shared journey in a supportive community, rather than a cutthroat battle for monetary rewards.

Business and Beyond

Most of these examples come from for-profit businesses, but gamification works equally well in social-impact contexts, in education, and

Figure 1.4: Kaggle User Profile

in scenarios where financial success isn't the default motivator. We'll see several examples in this book. The solution could also be a hybrid. The Chinese e-commerce giant Alibaba has incorporated a series of gamified social-impact mechanisms into its mobile applications. Users can open treasure boxes filled with "Sesame Seeds" that can be spent on donations to charitable projects, or they can nurture a virtual seedling until the company plants an actual tree in one of China's deforested regions. The philanthropy is real, but so is the improved retention as users return more frequently to the app.

The systems built by these organizations look very different from one another, and they operate in diverse contexts. But they are all examples of gamification and game thinking applied to business and social challenges.

Gamifi-what?

So what exactly is gamification? Companies have been applying game thinking to business challenges for some time without fully appreciating the scope of the concept. There are references to "gamifying" online systems as early as 1980. University of Essex professor Richard Bartle, a pioneer in multiplayer online games, says the word referred originally to "turning something not a game into a game."

The first use of gamification in its current sense apparently occurred in 2003, when Nick Pelling, a British game developer, established a short-lived consultancy to create game-like interfaces for electronic devices. The term fell into disuse, although during subsequent years, game designers such as Amy Jo Kim, Nicole Lazzaro, Jane McGonigal, and Ben Sawyer, as well as researchers such as Ian Bogost, James Paul Gee, and Byron Reeves, began to talk about the serious potential of video games. It was only in 2010, however, that the term "gamification" became widely adopted in the sense that people use it now.

Even now, the word "gamification" often draws blank stares or polite chuckles in conversations with executives. Gamification is a cumbersome word, and it doesn't capture the phenomenon in every respect. Many game developers and researchers worry—with good reason—that it trivializes the complexities of effective game design. Many gamification practitioners avoid a term that customers might find frivolous, and come up with various euphemisms for what they're doing. Regardless, "gamification" is the term that has stuck.

It's important to understand what gamification is not. It's not creating self-contained simulations that allow people to practice real-world activities. Nor is it game theory. If you're looking for the mathematical models immortalized in the movie *A Beautiful Mind*, you're in the wrong place.

Our working definition is the following:

Gamification: *The use of game elements and game-design techniques in non-game contexts.*

Let's break down this formulation and explain a little more about the three main aspects of the definition: game elements, game-design techniques, and non-game contexts.

Game Elements

A game manifests itself as an integrated experience, but it's built from many smaller pieces. We call those game elements. We'll go into more detail at Level 4, but for now, think of elements as a toolkit for building a game. Game elements for checkers, for example, include the pieces, the notion of capturing pieces by jumping, and turning a piece that reaches the last row of the board into a king. Notice that some of these are objects (the pieces), some are relationships among them (jumping), and some are abstract concepts embedding rules (making a king). In the Microsoft Language Quality Game, elements include the competition among international offices and the leaderboard allowing participants to compare their performance.

Just as you can assemble the same box of Legos into many kinds of objects, you can do different things with game elements. Most obviously, you can make a game. The game can be designed purely for fun (or associated revenue generation), or it can be designed to illustrate the complexities of the Israeli-Palestinian conflict. Or, you can assemble the elements into something that is not actually a game. When you're taking pieces of games and embedding them in business practices—challenging programmers to find bugs or having them guess search queries—you're engaged in gamification, and the end product is, one hopes, a better and more compelling business practice.

Remember that gamification isn't about building a full-fledged game. Because it operates at the level of elements, using gamification offers more flexibility. When you're playing checkers, you can't mess around with the game elements. If you did, the game wouldn't be checkers, would it? With gamification, though, bending the rules is exactly what you're called on to do. As the designer of a gamified system, you can and should tweak the elements to make the experience more engaging or to target certain business objectives. We'll talk about how you do this in later levels.

The key point is that game elements can be embedded into activities that are not themselves games. This radically expands the scope of opportunities.

The global consulting and auditing firm Deloitte realized that if it could get more of its consultants to share information about their client meetings on the corporate intranet, it would promote more efficient knowledge sharing and collaboration across the organization. Mere exhortations were unlikely to move these busy professionals to invest the time. A simulation game wouldn't do the trick, either. Deloitte needed to motivate, not educate.

Deloitte's solution was to harness game elements by adding a feature called WhoWhatWhere to its internal social messaging platform. It encourages consultants to "check in" with details about their meetings. Leaderboards track who has checked in the most with a client or topic. The leaders gain recognition and social currency in the organization as experts, and this recognition motivates participation. WhoWhatWhere is an example of applying the best parts of games without actually creating one. That's what gamification is.

Game-Design Techniques

Even though gamification isn't for making games, it still involves acting like a game designer. This can be deceptively tricky. It seems like no great challenge to take a game element such as a point system and stick it on a website: Want your customers to visit your website more often? Give them 100 points every time they check in! All it takes is a tiny bit of software code. And why not add a leaderboard? It's just a spreadsheet listing those points in rank order.

However, if you approach gamification in this way, you'll quickly run into trouble. What's the point of the points? Some users may find racking up a high score or topping the leaderboard inherently stimulating, at least for a while. But these users often get burned out by the endless treadmill of points accumulation and abandon the system. And most people don't find points particularly interesting. Many people look at the system and ask, "Why on earth should I care about this?" Even for the users who may care, the gamification design can be off-putting. New users may arrive with high hopes, only to abandon the system when they see the top of the leaderboard immensely far above them. These are just a few of the challenges you might encounter.

As we mentioned, the Redding *Record Searchlight* is a good example of how external gamification can generate customer engagement benefits. At one point, though, the editors got carried away and implemented a "deal finder" badge for readers who signed up to receive promotional emails. It was a spectacular failure. Users of the gamified site found the emails so annoying that subscriptions to the promo list actually went down after the badge system was implemented.

How do you decide which game elements to put where, and how to make the overall gamified experience greater than the sum of these parts? That's where game-design techniques come in. The aspects of games that make them fun, addicting, challenging, and emotionally resonant can't be reduced to step-by-step instructions, but there are some time-honored best practices. Game design is a bit of science, a bit of art, and a lot of hard-won experience—just like strategic leadership, managing a team, or creating a killer marketing campaign.

Game design is hard. Even great game designers, like great film directors, sometimes produce poor-quality works. Successful companies such as Electronic Arts and Sony have spent tens of millions of dollars on online games that flopped. If you don't appreciate the accumulated knowledge and time-tested techniques of good game design, though, your chances of failure are far greater. That's why, in this book, we spend at least as much time on the "how" and "why" of gamification as we do on the "what."

Non-game Contexts

The final aspect of our definition is that gamification operates in non-game contexts. As noted earlier, this can mean internal, external, behavior-change, or crowdsourcing situations. The key element in each is that they involve real-world goals. Your players are not storming a castle; they are exploring the website of your TV show or solving an innovation challenge for your firm. They are not killing dragons; they are collecting achievements on the way to improving their financial situation or learning a new subject. This is important to keep in mind when designing a gamified system. Your players aren't there to escape from your product into a fantasy world; they are there to engage more deeply with your product or business or objective. Those Accenture employees weren't hacking apart goblins; they were learning not to leave their laptops vulnerable to theft while traveling. Yet somehow, magically, it still *felt* like a game.

The challenge of gamification, therefore, is to take the elements that normally operate within the game universe and apply them effectively in the real world. In an array of situations, organizations are finding that gamification produces measurable results.

Nike has done something similar with its Nike+ loyalty program. Runners can visually track their progress, compare themselves with others, receive real-time encouragement from friends, complete challenges, earn achievements, and unlock rewards. The system improves the experience of running and ties sneakers into an online community that keeps customers returning to buy Nike shoes whenever their old ones wear out.

Taking Games Seriously

As a final point, we want to directly confront the question that's likely in your head or in the heads of those you discuss the concept with: *Why should a practice based on games be taken seriously?*

There are several good answers to this question. If you've read this far, chances are you can already think of some. We see three particularly compelling reasons why every organization should at least consider gamification:

- Engagement
- Experimentation
- Results

Engagement

The most basic answer is that gamification is about engagement. The same human needs that drive people to play games are present in the workplace, the marketplace, school, volunteering, and pretty much any serious context that comes to mind. Think of gamification as a means to design systems that motivate people to do things. Anything that makes your target community more motivated to engage will be good for your business.

The reason for this is simple. It turns out that our brains are wired to crave puzzle solving, feedback and reinforcement, and the other experiences that games provide. Study after study has shown that games activate the brain's dopamine system, which is associated with pleasure. Neuroscientists have also found intriguing parallels between the brain's response to games and the process of inquiry. As renowned game designer Raph Koster writes: "With games, learning is the drug." What executive wouldn't want to harness the natural high that motivates learning and higher levels of engagement?

As we'll discuss, there's a danger in focusing too much on this pleasure-seeking reward dynamic as the basis for gamification. Just as drugs can make you happy for a while but eventually become counterproductive, gamification should draw on more than the brain's most primitive systems. A well-designed, nuanced gamification system can give you a powerful set of tools to develop challenges for your customers and employees that are meaningful and intrinsically engaging.

Engagement has business value in itself. In 2019, the annual survey on engagement by Gallup found that 85% of workers worldwide weren't fully engaged in their jobs. This undoubtedly affects not only their performance but also their happiness. People know they should exercise more, eat better, get regular health checkups, conserve energy, and so forth; the hard part is being sufficiently motivated to do so. And for consumers, engagement is what leads them to initiate a transaction. In some cases the benefits are indirect. Perhaps you want to engender camaraderie among your employees. Or maybe you want to persuade a large number of strangers to tackle a collective problem, like studying NASA photographs to locate interesting new planets that automated systems can't find. Or maybe you want to identify your best customers, who have an outsize impact on your bottom line.

Experimentation

A second powerful aspect of game-based motivation is to open up the space of possibility. Mastering a game is all about experimentation. You expect to experience some failure, but because you can always start over, failure doesn't feel so daunting. In most video games, you may win, but you can never permanently lose. If the game is effective—not too difficult, never too easy—players are continually motivated to strive for improvement. And they are encouraged to try new and different approaches, even crazy ones, to find better solutions. That ethos of constant innovation is perfectly suited for today's fast-moving business environment.

Experimenting with the lessons in this book can pay dividends beyond gamification. As table 1.1 shows, game elements are already present in the real world. We just don't think about them in that way. News coverage of political campaigns and legislative battles often uses game language and imagery. Ask young people today how they see school, their relationship with brands, and their jobs, and they are quite likely to describe them in terms that sound eerily game-like. The throwaway line that life, or work, is "just a game" rings strangely true.

The fact is that there's significant overlap between work, school, consumer interactions, and games. Sure, some people spend every moment of the workday waiting for it to end. Similarly, some coldly

Table 1.1: Game Concepts in the Real World

Real-World Activity	Game Concept
Monthly sales competition	Challenge
Frequent-flier program tiers	Levels
Weight Watchers group	Team
Free coffee after 10 purchases at Starbucks	Reward
American Express platinum card	Badge

appraise their choice of products (such as cars) based on price, features, and styling. Yet we've all heard of people who love their jobs and those who love their cars. If that doesn't sound strange, why resist the notion that games offer a pathway to improve experiences with business or social objectives?

Related to this, you may have come across "serious games" before. Chances are that the pilot of your last flight and the surgeon who operated on you trained with specialized 3-D simulation games. There are substantial communities building games for health, military applications, environmental awareness, corporate training, and education, among other categories. There's even a remarkable public school in New York City, Quest to Learn, built entirely around games. In a slightly different vein, many games are designed to achieve marketing or advertising objectives, such as the annual Monopoly Game at McDonald's or the branded interactive games you'll often find on customer-facing business websites. Such advergames are now standard operating procedure for advertising and interactive agencies.

As we see things, serious games and their ilk are special cases of gamification. They are examples of using game design in non-game contexts by assembling game elements into full-blown games. There are substantial communities today around these practices, with their own books and conferences. Some of our examples, such as Neofect's Rapael glove and Accenture's information security training, might qualify as serious games. Even there, the point isn't to immerse players in the experience. Most of the examples in this book don't even have such game-like visual interfaces. Our primary focus in this book is on embedding game elements into existing practices, from exercise regimens to corporate innovation programs.

The rise of e-commerce, online communications tools in the workplace, mobile devices, and social media makes these experiences increasingly game-like. The similarities between the interfaces of Wall Street trading terminals, enterprise collaboration software, and online games are too striking to ignore.

Results

There's a final reason you should be interested in gamification: *It works*. Many companies have seen significant positive results from incorporating game elements into their business processes. And not just exotic start-ups. In this chapter alone we've discussed Microsoft, Accenture, Nike, and Deloitte, which are just a few of the leading global firms employing gamification techniques. They aren't doing so just because they think it's cool.

When we originally published *For the Win*, the case for gamification was mostly anecdotal. There are now hundreds of peer-reviewed academic journal articles showing how the approach can succeed. For example, a gamified training program for radiologists reduced error rates significantly, from 39% to 22%. That could make a big difference if it's your X-ray being analyzed for a medical condition! Overall, 87% of the radiologists described the experience as fun, and 93% said they would use the training software again.

A survey published in 2019 found that in 75% of controlled empirical studies, gamification had either positive or mostly positive effects. A separate review of 91 papers on gamification of education found a similar success rate. The percentages aren't higher because, as we'll see, gamification solutions need to be designed well to be effective. Many studies evaluate gamification attempts that fail because they violate the principles we cover in this book. As we'll discuss, one lesson from games is that failure itself can be a learning experience.

If you haven't already, it's time to get into the game!

Game Thinking
Learning to Think Like a Game Designer

> *Games are nature's most beautiful creation.*
> —Leonard Cohen

At Level 1, we identified some situations in which gamification can make a difference in business, and we gave you some important definitions. Now, to level you up, we explain the basic features of games and game thinking so that you can begin to recognize how to put game thinking to work in your projects and determine whether gamification can deliver the results you need.

We'll answer the following questions:

- *What is fun, and what is a game?*
- *Why should I think like a game designer, and how do I do it?*
- *What sort of business problems can be gamified?*
- *How do I start?*

The world's deepest trash can used to sit in a park in Sweden. It looked like any other trash can. But when park visitors dropped a piece of trash into it, they heard the whistling sound of an object falling for a very, very long distance, followed by a satisfying "bong!" as it hit the bottom. Candid videos of park visitors show them looking startled and confused initially, then smiling with delight at something so unexpected. Later videos show visitors roaming the park grounds, looking for trash to drop into the can.

No enterprising Scandinavian elves dug a deep hole for the magical trash can. Instead, a group of engineers created a simple motion detector and speaker system that they installed in the lid of a regular bin. Trash dropped into the bin actually fell about three feet, but the speakers mimicked the sound of it falling hundreds of feet. The idea of this experiment was to answer a question: Would people drop more trash into a bin if it were fun? The answer is yes, indeed. The amount of trash deposited in the gamified trash can was almost twice that of a regular park bin sitting nearby.

The trash can was part of a Volkswagen initiative called the Fun Theory, which sought to use fun to change people's behaviors. The Fun Theory also created bottle bank recyclers that looked like slot machines; a lottery for drivers who *didn't* speed, with a prize pool drawn from fines levied on those who did; and, most famously, a project called Piano Stairs (figure 2.1), featured in a YouTube video that has been seen over 23 million times.

We all know that using the stairs is good exercise, but most people prefer the comfort of an escalator. The Fun Theory turned the

Figure 2.1: The Fun Theory's Piano Stairs

stairs at a Stockholm subway station into a huge electronic piano, with each step corresponding to a key that made an audible sound. The result: 66% more people took the stairs. The video shows many of them bouncing up and down, transported by the joy found in making such unexpected music. Those stair climbers did something good for themselves, and they had fun in the process.

And if you need another example of how fun can be used to create amazing outcomes, consider the ALS Association Ice Bucket Challenge, which swept the internet in 2014. The concept was simple: Challenge your friends to record a video dumping a bucket of ice over their (or someone else's) head. Fun, huh? Lots of people thought so. In the end, 17 million participants took the challenge. It went viral because it was hilarious to see friends and family reacting to the shock of the ice water, and the creative ways people implemented the challenge. The kicker was that in conjunction with recording the video, participants were encouraged to donate to the ALS Association. Those videos raised $115 million for medical research on ALS, a degenerative muscular disease.

It shouldn't come as a surprise to see that fun motivates people. Gamification is the process of manipulating fun to serve real-world objectives. Fun, though, is a slippery concept, and there isn't much value in trying to define it in the abstract. Instead, we want to teach you how to deploy fun in a considered and directed way that leads to real results. This is called "game thinking."

When both of us were in law school, we were often told that the objective of the program was to enable us to "think like a lawyer." Sure, we learned the hearsay rules of evidence, but the enduring takeaway was an analytical approach that could be applied in virtually any situation. Similarly, to be effective at gamification, you need to think like a game designer. If you do, you'll find the fun in all sorts of business problems and come up with solutions that naturally engage people and motivate them to do the things that you want.

But how do you start? To help you begin to think like a game designer, we start by asking an essential question . . .

What's in a Game?

First things first: We need to define what we mean by a game. You undoubtedly have an idea of what a game is. However, coming up with a precise definition is surprisingly difficult. What unites Monopoly, football, Animal Crossing, bridge, Pac-Man, and duck, duck, goose?

You might think at first that fun is a necessary feature. But not all games seem like fun, nor is everything fun a game. (Watching *Game of Thrones* is fun, but it's not a game.) Are there other features that are found in all games? What about the typical features of games—teams, for instance? Well, not all games have teams. What about winning and losing? Well, not all games involve . . . you get the idea. It's almost impossible to define any essential attribute of games. The philosopher Ludwig Wittgenstein actually used the difficulty of adequately defining games to illustrate some knotty philosophical problems.

Have no fear, that's the last you'll hear of Wittgenstein in this book. For gamified business applications, all we need is a good enough understanding of games to be useful in developing real-world systems. One important aspect is that games are voluntary—no one can force you to have fun. As NYU divinity scholar James P. Carse said, "Whoever must play, cannot play." Second, games require those who play to make choices, and those choices have consequences that produce feedback. The choices may involve picking a weapon in a video game or playing a particular word in Scrabble. Those decisions affect your experience playing the game. In fact, Sid Meier, legendary designer of the Civilization series of games, defined a game as simply "a series of meaningful choices."

Contingent choices highlight the connection between games and autonomy. Players feel a sense of control in games that is deeply empowering. We'll return to this concept in several places. Even more essential, though, is the fact that games seem somehow *different* from mundane reality. A game player who is sitting in an ordinary chair, in an ordinary office, doing an ordinary job can experience a pull that seems to originate somewhere else. That's what can make a gamified customer engagement system more effective than, say, a coupon or a "10% off" promotion.

Why is it that games take us outside our mundane life, even when nothing really has changed? The early twentieth-century Dutch thinker Johan Huizinga introduced the concept of the "magic circle." The magic circle is the imaginary space that separates a game from the rest of the world. Players of a game step into the magic circle, and so voluntarily suspend the rules of the real world and accept the rules of the game. It doesn't matter if the boundary is physical or virtual; what matters is that players accept that the game is *real* to them in some way. A game has some rules, some objectives, and some obstacles to overcome in order to achieve those objectives—but the crucial element is the players' willingness to accept all those things and conform their behavior to them.

To state it briefly: A game is what happens in the magic circle.

Here are a couple of simple ways to understand what it means to be inside and outside the magic circle. Think of walking onto a football field as the quarterback. By doing so you accept the risks of injury of a (legal) tackle by a defensive player, because you're *inside the magic circle*. But the magic circle is more than the mere field where play takes place. If, after the game is over, you are standing on the exact same gridiron and someone (like the late former Philadelphia Eagles player Chuck "Concrete Charlie" Bednarik, who played for the Penn Quakers in college) tackles you, you would sue them for assault and battery. Because after the game is over, you are outside the magic circle, even if you're on the field.

Think of the power of the magic circle in a business context. You create a "world" to serve your strategic objectives, and it becomes meaningful to other people such as visitors to your website, the people using your app, or your staff in the call center. They are pulled toward the goals you've defined, not because you've forced them to be, but because they are within the magic circle and so they want to be playing your game, by your rules. Creating a gamified experience like this is hard, and it comes with a set of responsibilities. The rest of this book is about all the complexities involved in effective gamification. The potential, though, is quite extraordinary—not only will people join you in meeting your business purpose, *they will enjoy it!*

If you're worried that building an effective game is an unfamiliar challenge requiring specialized skills, don't be. Gamification uses game thinking and elements, and it requires some practice—but it doesn't necessarily involve creating an actual game. Think back to the ALS Ice Bucket Challenge. It was a simple idea, without all the trappings of a game. But it motivated millions to raise money for a great cause. Use this example as your starting point, and jump in. What you already know about your business and your customers will get you most of the way to building a great gamified experience. All you need are the tools and methods to create game-like experiences for your users.

Game Thinking

Now that we know a bit about games, let's talk about game thinking. To do gamification well, you need to learn to think a little like a game designer. This doesn't mean *being* a game designer. We're not asking you to build storyboards, 3-D models, physics engines, or any of the things that go into modern video games. And frankly, some examples of gamification are only game-like in the vaguest sense. Game thinking is a way to approach your existing business challenges in the same tradition as total quality management, process reengineering, design thinking, or any other business technique.

Compare game thinking with learning how to drive a car. You can read a book about what all the pedals and levers do, and you can learn the traffic rules in your jurisdiction. But no matter how much studying you do, the first time you sit behind the wheel and turn the key, you'll feel uncomfortable and probably be a danger to those on the road around you.

There's a reason no one becomes a good driver without actually practicing driving, usually with an instructor in the car: Descriptions can never make you think like a driver. Knowing what appropriate acceleration feels like on the gas pedal, what to make of that car changing lanes in front of you, and whether to stop when the light turns yellow are bits of situated knowledge that experienced drivers internalize. And just as novice drivers have to practice driving, you will need to practice game design to become a good practitioner of the art and science of gamification.

Game thinking means using all the resources you can muster to create an engaging experience that motivates the behaviors that you want your users to display. There will be huge benefits to this: Some of the things that games do well include encouraging problem solving, sustaining interest as users move from novice to expert to master, breaking down big challenges into manageable steps, promoting teamwork, giving participants a sense of control, personalizing the experience to each person, rewarding out-of-the-box thinking, reducing the fear of failure that inhibits innovative experimentation, supporting diverse interests and skill sets, and cultivating a confident, optimistic attitude. All this from the sole practice of game thinking.

Think of an objective you are facing—maybe it's improving customer retention in your business, or maybe you want more clients to renew their insurance policies, or perhaps you want more repeat buyers on your online fashion site. Traditional approaches to these problems would be to refresh your marketing campaigns, look at your pricing practices, adjust your value proposition, or pore over your customer metrics looking for a piece of useful data.

Game thinking asks a different question: Why do people buy your product or use your service in the first place? And it asks it in a particular way: What is their motivation? What makes your customers *want* to do business with you? And once you know this, game thinking asks: Can you make it more compelling, more interesting, and more fun? Even if your business involves a bloodless exchange of money for value provided, approaching your business problem with game thinking can transform the entire way you engage with your customers, staff, and users. Think back to our initial example of the world's deepest trash can. The game designers of the Fun Theory took something incredibly boring—throwing away trash—and turned it into something compelling. You can do the same thing in your business.

Notice that we're not asking you to think like a gamer. We all play games, and so we already think like gamers. For some of us, the games have names such as Candy Crush or Apex Legends; for others they are golf, Scrabble, or Texas Hold'em; and for others they are "acquire more Facebook friends," "close enough deals to get that trip to Bermuda," or "ace the GMAT exam." When you're engaged in a game that you care about, you naturally try to succeed, whether that means vanquishing your rivals or earning the admiration of your friends. Evolution has wired our brains to be natural game-playing machines.

But playing a game is very different from understanding what it takes to create an effective game experience. Applying gamification to solve business or other non-game problems puts you in the role of the game designer, not the game player. That's not nearly as intuitive to most people, and that's what we're here to teach you.

The first lesson of game thinking is this: Gamers want to win, while game designers want to make gamers play. It's a subtle but important distinction. If you build an effective gamified system, your players—whether they're employees, customers, or some other group—will attempt to hit the targets the game offers them. You, on the other hand, care about those targets only as a proxy for other things. Maybe you want your community members to reduce their carbon footprint, or maybe you want your consultants to share more information about clients with coworkers. Your baseline goal is to get your players playing and keep them playing. Only then can they generate the desired business benefits.

Now, let's take this first lesson and start you thinking like a game designer. Why do you think that so many video games involve levels? Players start at Level 1 and work their way up through increasingly more challenging stages. Reaching a new level is an accomplishment that gamers call "leveling up." Leveling up signifies progress, and progress feels good. To crib a phrase from former Apple CEO John Sculley, the journey becomes the reward.

Our second lesson is this: Progress matters. How you create that sense of progress will differ. Sometimes you will find that without levels players can lose interest because they have no measurable sense of progress. Of course, you don't have to explicitly use levels to generate a sense of progression—open-world games can create the feeling through an increase in skill sets or through the acquisition of items that unlock certain types of gameplay. Even "sandbox games"—like The Sims or Minecraft, which encourage players to explore or build a world with no predefined objectives—still need dynamism and growth, either in the world itself or in the player's mastery of the objectives. Otherwise these games quickly become static, stagnant, and boring. Even if some games have clear goals, the *playing* of games is a process, not an outcome.

Notice that we've been using the word "players." From now on, we will employ that term to refer to the participants in any gamified system, whether they happen to be your customers, your employees, your partners, or your user community. This matters. Just thinking about these people as "players" can have salutary effects on how you design for them, for the same reason the department store giant Target studiously calls its customers "guests" and its employees "team members."

So this is your third lesson: Start to think of the people you are designing for as players. And never forget that your players are the center of the game and that they need to have a sense of being in control. After all, players pick the game; the game doesn't pick them. The excitement of the experience comes, as we've noted, partly from the players' sense of autonomy.

Bear in mind, though, that a player's sense of autonomy is always illusory. The game designer makes the rules and the game enforces them. This is especially true in digital games, where so much happens through the software code that players never see. But every game has rules, and these constrain the players within the game. You can't build a condominium in Monopoly, even if you want to; the rules say that you're limited to houses and hotels. That's true in business as well. Nike's customers can't design any shoe they want; they are limited to the choices Nike offers them. By offering more options for individual customization, though, Nike promotes a sense of empowerment. That's the secret to its successful Nike By You custom shoe co-creation program, which lets buyers select personalized designs for every portion of the shoe.

If you think of your customers, and even your employees, as players in a game you operate, you're more likely to identify opportunities to give them meaningful choices.

Is Gamification Right for My Challenge?

Gamification isn't a solution to every problem. Now that you've put yourself in the role of game designer, you should ask whether gamification makes sense for the challenges you hope to address.

Start by accepting that some things just aren't fun: A funeral home probably wouldn't want to gamify the buying process for a loved one's coffin. But it's equally important to recognize that some things are naturally fun, and thus there is no need to gamify them. You might play a game such as three-legged race at the company picnic, but you probably wouldn't want to gamify the picnic itself. The picnic is an example of undirected play. Turning it into a structured process would do more harm than good. In other words, gamification works for concrete business objectives that aren't fun themselves but can be made fun using gamification techniques.

Imagine that your local supermarket chain wants to implement gamification. It looks at its business and quickly concludes that some aspects are more amenable to gamification than others. It doesn't want the employees stocking produce to feel angry or dissatisfied with their jobs, but it's not clear how much its business would profit if those employees were super passionate. It may not be worth the investment to gamify this part of the business. On the other hand, engaged consumers are more likely to go out of their way to shop at their favorite store, will buy more, and will be evangelists for the business. Of course, having a sale can motivate customers, but price cuts eat into the bottom line, can be matched by competitors, and don't necessarily make for engaged customers. A gamified system to increase the engagement and loyalty of regular supermarket shoppers makes a great deal of sense for this business need.

Let's define the process more systematically. To figure out where gamification might be used in your business, consider the following four core questions:

1. **Motivation:** Can you solve a business problem by encouraging certain types of behavior?
2. **Meaningful choices:** Are your target activities interesting?
3. **Structure:** Can the desired behaviors be modeled through a set of rules?
4. **Potential conflicts:** Can the game avoid conflicts with existing motivational approaches?

Motivation: Where Would You Derive Value from Encouraging Behavior?

Gamification is a form of motivational design, as we'll discuss in more detail in Level 3. It is fundamentally a means to get people to behave in a certain way. If your problem is a lack of qualified programmers in your organization, or that buyers consider your prices too high, then you might think that gamification is unlikely to offer much in the way of solutions. However, if you reconceive of the problem in terms of motivation—"How can we attract more talented programmers even though our city isn't a tech hub?" or "How can we motivate our customers to pay our prices even though they may not seem competitive at first?"—then you are well on the way to becoming an excellent gamification designer.

There are three main kinds of activities for which motivation is particularly important: creative work, mundane tasks, and behavior change. Some tasks involve emotional connections, unique skills, creativity, and teamwork. These are the high-value-added activities or customer relationships that make an outsize contribution to competitive advantage. They are also great candidates for gamification.

Whether it's designing a new product or nurturing high-profile brand ambassadors, such tasks depend heavily on having highly motivated people. They work best when people are deeply engaged and focused—hopefully even passionate—about what they are doing. Gamification can give them a satisfying, individualized, ongoing rewarding experience unlike anything else.

At the other end of the spectrum are mundane tasks that involve adherence to defined procedures and that are purely individual in nature. Creativity shouldn't be high on the list when one is hiring auditors, for example. Gamification can, however, be effective in these situations, but it needs to be done differently. Your goal is not to trick people into tolerating a boring task; it's to help them find a measure of meaning in the activity.

Take physical rehabilitation as an example. People who suffer a stroke have to go through painful and grueling therapy to retrain their brains and muscles so that they can move comfortably again. It's a tough process. In conjunction with physical tracking devices, the South Korean company Neofect, which we noted in the introduction, uses gamification techniques to provide its patients with the motivation they need to keep working on the movements of their hands and arms. With gamified visualizations—users throw darts at an imaginary board or carefully pour imaginary wine into a glass—along with a social community support function, Neofect clients have logged over 95,000 hours of home rehab use, with numerous success stories.

Finally, there are behavior-change scenarios in which people understand that something is good for them but have a hard time doing it. The challenge is to make the activity habitual. The obvious example is fitness and exercise, which is a tough sell for most of us, even though we know we should be doing it. This sector is one that has been transformed by gamification since we wrote the first edition of this book: Numerous fitness trackers and exercise apps use gamification these days, in a range of ways.

Strava motivates players to run or cycle by allowing virtual competitions between friends. Fitbit encourages users to get healthy by setting daily goals for number of steps taken and hours slept, with a range of feedback loops to push users toward their goals. These are only two examples within a very crowded sector: A 2017 study of gamification in health and fitness apps showed that nearly 80% of these apps used goal setting or social influencing to motivate users, and around 60% used challenges to motivate them. This is gamification at its most obvious.

Meaningful Choices: Are Your Target Activities Interesting?

Successful gamified processes require players to feel they have autonomy, whether that's consumers deciding to purchase or workers deciding to take actions beyond their job requirements. Players can't just be following a predefined track. When they realize there's no inherent reason to care, any engagement bump they experience from game mechanics will be fleeting.

Meaningful choices simply mean options that give the player some freedom of choice, so that noticeable consequences flow from those decisions. In World of Warcraft, for example, a player can choose from several character classes, each of which has different strengths and weaknesses. WeSpire is a gamified platform provider that works with companies to motivate their employees to choose positive behaviors. Its tool offers a large range of choices for employees, whether it be volunteering at pet shelters, skipping food delivery and cooking at home more, reducing water usage, or recycling more. Even though all these options serve the goals of the platform and the user's employer, they give the user a sense of autonomy. A gamified system that offers rewards but no choices will quickly feel disempowering and boring for most players.

Structure: Can the Desired Behaviors Be Understood Through a Set of Rules?

Games unleash the ineffable quality of fun, but gamification requires rules and algorithms to measure and respond to actions. Also, you will likely want to record or track player activities, so this will mean implementing algorithms and an online system to manage the game.

One of the first examples of this in action came from the consumer electronics giant Samsung, which gamified its website with a program called Samsung Nation in 2011. Players could earn badges and level up by reviewing products, watching videos, and providing responses for product Q&As. To operationalize this, Samsung built a point system that assigned a value for each action—for example, sharing an action on Twitter was worth 100 points, and registering a Samsung product you bought was worth 500. This way, the company could use algorithms to run the game and produce rewards.

The gamified Samsung site is gone now, but many companies today have similarly gamified websites and processes. The lesson here is not about Samsung's success or even the value of points (something we will talk about in Level 3). It's about the importance of having some way to model options algorithmically. A point system is one way, but you need to think about whether there are any rules that you can use for your problem. If you are looking to use gamification to encourage innovation in your organization, then you need a structured way to assess, say, the difference between a high-quality innovation and a poor one. If you don't have this—and you likely won't, because innovation is impossible to assess like this—then gamification isn't likely to be a good means of motivating innovation in your organization.

Potential Conflicts: Can the Game Avoid Interfering with Existing Motivational Approaches?

As we'll discuss in Level 4, studies show that game mechanics such as leaderboards can actually demotivate workers when the mechanic is entangled with traditional rewards like salary and bonuses. When they see how low they are in the standings, many workers will give up. The climb up the ladder is too daunting.

Similarly, if your promise to customers is that you'll save them time and help them become more efficient, a gamified offering that encourages them to waste time in a seemingly frivolous activity may generate cognitive dissonance.

It's important to identify all the existing ways you motivate your target population and to think through how they would function alongside gamification. Put yourself in the shoes of a player and ask what message your organization is sending. There isn't necessarily a conflict. The example of WeSpire is a useful lesson. Many people are altruistic and would like to recycle more or volunteer to deliver food to elderly people amid the COVID-19 pandemic. WeSpire's gamified platform doesn't automatically eliminate people's desire to do these things. However, WeSpire carefully structures and positions its game elements to avoid sending the message that the users' altruistic acts are financial transactions or somehow trivial.

Pulling It Together

You can think of the previous four questions as *design goals*. The ideal candidates for gamification are processes that depend on motivation, offer interesting challenges that are easily coded into rules, and reinforce existing reward systems. In reality, things don't always fall into place so nicely. The four questions are not either/or. In other words, the more meaningful the choices, the better.

In Level 4, we will discuss the specific gamification elements you can use in your project. But don't jump straight to these elements. Instead, approach your project as an integrated design exercise and begin by filling out a chart such as table 2.1. For a hypothetical supermarket gamification initiative, the chart would look something like table 2.2.

Table 2.1: Basic Gamification Table

Players		Frameworks		
Activity	1. Motivation	2. Meaningful Choices	3. Structure	4. Potential Conflicts

Table 2.2: Completed Checklist for Supermarket Example

Players		Frameworks		
Activity	1. Motivation	2. Meaningful Choices	3. Structure	4. Potential Conflicts
Check-out clerk performance	Not clear that engagement would improve customer experience	Largely noncreative activity	Average time of customer checkout easy to measure	Perhaps intrinsic enjoyment can be added to a dull activity, but gamification might produce resentment
Shopper loyalty rewards	Give customers a reason to choose us other than price and in-store service, with direct revenue benefits	Let customers choose how to qualify for different kinds of rewards	Purchases automatically tracked through our POS system and loyalty cards	Customer and company interests aligned

Note: *An X indicates that the criterion does not support use of gamification for the activity. A partial X indicates that the criterion might support gamification, but is unlikely to do so.*

Before thinking about specific gamification elements, you'll want to resolve each block of the chart in a positive way. In other words, you need a strong answer for how you meet each requirement or your project will be lacking in some crucial way. As your thinking evolves, go back and modify your answers. Then evaluate how changes in one box affect the others. You should do this before you make any decisions about the specifics of your system. It's much easier to make changes and avoid mistakes at this conceptual stage.

Level 3

Why Games Work
The Rules of Motivation

> *A soldier will fight long and hard for a bit of colored ribbon.*
> —Napoleon Bonaparte

You've seen how gamification can work in general (Level 1) and how to assess whether your business issue is amenable to gamification (Level 2). Now we get to talk about your players and what makes them tick.

We'll ask the following questions:

- *What does research tell us about psychology and motivation?*
- *What are extrinsic and intrinsic motivators, and how can I use them?*
- *How do I motivate behavior through gamification?*

What does the ESP Game, the "I am not a robot" test on websites, and the world's largest community of language learners have in common?

Two things, actually: gamification and Luis von Ahn.

Von Ahn is a professor of computer science at Carnegie Mellon University and a winner of the MacArthur "Genius" Award at 28. He's also the creator of Duolingo, the world's most successful language learning app and one of the most well-known examples of gamification (figure 3.1). Duolingo encourages players to learn languages using a slew of gamification techniques, like points, achievements,

Figure 3.1: Duolingo

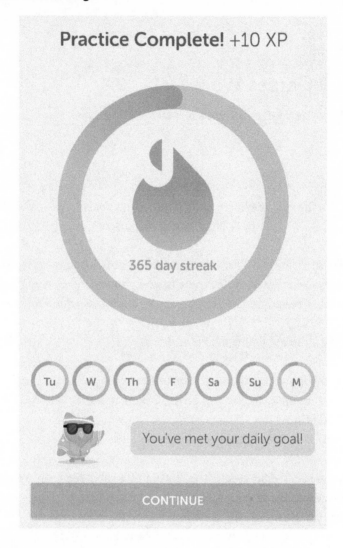

leaderboards, strong feedback loops, content unlocking, and social engagement. (That's to say nothing of a cute green owl who will badger you to death if you don't learn your conjugations.)

For those who have read our companion book, *The Gamification Toolkit*, you'll remember we talked briefly about Duolingo. It has grown massively in the years since, and it has also upped its gamifi-cation game. Its success, by now, is obvious—it offers 94 different lan-guage courses in 23 languages, has over 300 million registered users, and counts Google's parent company as one of its investors—but the story of its development is much more interesting.

Before creating Duolingo with his graduate student Severin Hacker, von Ahn had pioneered gamification elements in unexpected areas. For example, he created the internet-based ESP Game, where two randomly paired players are given the same photo to describe and are awarded points if their descriptions match. What seems like a fun game—"What are the best words to describe this photo so that my description matches my co-player's?"—is, in fact, a way to have human beings tag photos to improve Google search results. The same is true of the reCAPTCHA system that von Ahn pio-neered (and Google later purchased). Not only is it a way for web-sites to ensure that you are not a robot, but this system is also a way of having human beings label text and photos that cannot easily be interpreted by computers. Early versions of reCAPTCHA solved the optical character recognition problem for the *New York Times* archive. Later ones have deciphered roadside features like stop signs, pedestrian crossings, and traffic lights to train self-driving cars.

Duolingo, the ESP Game, and reCAPTCHA are all examples of how gamified elements can be used to get people to do things that they otherwise find too onerous. In this sense, they are like the gam-ified apps we find in health and fitness that motivate people to get off their couches and into physical activity. Using GPS-enabled mobile apps, you can compete in virtual bike races against your friends in Strava, or try to outrun imaginary zombies as you jog along your favorite path using Zombies, Run! (figure 3.2).

Gamification can make us do things we wouldn't otherwise con-sider. Now that you're at Level 3, you're ready to explore what moti-vates people to do things, and thus you can start to think about what your players will enjoy and how you can get them to do the things that you need them to do.

Figure 3.2: Zombies, Run!

What Makes People Tick

The word "motivation" comes from the Latin *motivus*, meaning "serving to move." To be motivated is to be moved to do something. People are like objects: They have a certain inertia that needs to be overcome for them to get on with things.

Let's say that you don't have any particular desire to see the latest Amy Schumer movie. Psychologists call that being "amotivated." It's not necessarily a comment on the movie; plenty of people pay $15 to go and watch it. So why do they go? Many reasons, of course, but a simple division for those going to the movie is between those who *want* to see Amy Schumer and those who feel like they *have* to go see her. *Wanting* to do something is called "intrinsic" motivation because, for the person involved, it lies inside them or the activity. On the other hand, feeling that you *need* to do something involves "extrinsic" motivation, because the motivation lies outside.

Exercising is another example. Many people don't exercise, and so they are amotivated. On the other hand, those who do exercise may be intrinsically motivated or extrinsically motivated to do so. People who like exercise and feel better afterward have intrinsic motivation. People whose doctors tell them they have to exercise for health reasons are extrinsically motivated.

The distinction between intrinsic and extrinsic motivation may seem abstract, but it's critically important. Hundreds of peer-reviewed academic articles and scores of real-world case studies demonstrate why it matters whether intrinsic or extrinsic motivation is the basis for action. In general, intrinsic motivation is stronger, better, and a longer-lasting way of changing people's behavior. So, what's the difference?

Imagine you don't have any desire to go see Amy Schumer, but your spouse and kids do, or your theater has a promotion offering free popcorn, or a lot of your friends or family are talking about the movie. Along the same lines, you may not want to prepare the annual budget at work. But it's your job. Or, you study for your statistics exam because you won't graduate without passing the class. These are extrinsic motivators. What's motivating you comes from outside your enjoyment or engagement with the activity.

We've all experienced extrinsic motivation. It's hard to overstate its importance in the business world and our daily lives. Many employees—perhaps most—turn up to work because they are being paid to do so and will lose their jobs if they don't. They may sometimes find enjoyment in doing a good job or mastering a task, but it's the exception rather than the rule. Salespeople work longer and harder than they would otherwise because their end-of-year bonus is dependent on sales. Employees know that if they get a bad performance review, they won't get promoted. Carrots and sticks are so common in employment that we tend to assume they are the only way to motivate behavior. Yet that's not the case.

Think about activities you really, really want to do. You would do them without any hope of payment or other external benefits. Every person is different, but a typical list of activities would include socializing with friends, spending quality time with your spouse and/or family, playing sports, eating and sleeping, reading, walking along a beach at sunset, watching television, or playing video games.

Ask yourself *why* you want to do these things and you will find that there are lots of different reasons: Being with and providing for your family is something that is part of your foundational sense of self as a person. Eating and sleeping are needs you have as a human being. Success in sports or work can promote feelings of competency and achievement. Walking along the beach and watching television are activities that are enjoyable and relaxing. These are all intrinsically motivated activities.

Activities do not fall into these categories in and of themselves. Motivation involves an interaction between a person and a task, in a situation and at a time. Remember the Amy Schumer movie example? You may have no strong feelings one way or the other about it. (You're amotivated.) Your neighbor, though, goes to see it because her husband promised her a fancy dinner afterward. (She's extrinsically motivated.) Her husband wants to go because he's a comedy aficionado and thinks Amy Schumer is great. (He's intrinsically motivated.) Of course, some tasks are more likely to fall into one category or the other—taking out the trash is something that most people don't find intrinsically motivating.

What goes for Amy Schumer movies also goes for getting customers to buy, helping students stay on track in their studies, engaging workers, and any other objectives for a gamification project. In the following sections, we pull apart the various features of intrinsic and extrinsic motivation, show how gamification can be used to motivate, and demonstrate risks when gamification practitioners don't understand motivation.

The Rules of Motivation

Psychologists have been studying how to get people to do things for quite some time. In the second half of the twentieth century, the dominant theory was known as behaviorism. This approach sought to explain behavior purely based on external responses to stimuli. The best-known studies were done by Ivan Pavlov on his famous salivating dogs, and by B. F. Skinner, whose infamous "Skinner boxes" gave food or electric shocks to pigeons and rats. So-called behaviorist studies like these examined the reinforcement effects of reward and punishment on the behavior of animals and extrapolated the lessons to humans. The basic idea was that humans and animals responded to external stimuli and changed their behavior in predictable ways.

Behaviorist thinking suggested that extrinsic motivation was always the way to get people to do things. A reward or punishment, systematically applied, would reinforce responses in anticipation of further rewards or punishments. Indeed, this is reflected in the standard business motivation methods of that era (and maybe ours). Think of the rewards of salary and bonuses, and the punishments of demotion or firing. All very neat and industrial.

Against this behaviorist approach are a collection of "cognitivist" theories of motivation that ask what's actually going on in people's heads when they decide to do or not do things. Perhaps the most influential of these theories is the Self-Determination Theory (SDT) of Edward Deci, Richard Ryan, and their collaborators. Deci and Ryan suggest that human beings are inherently proactive, with a strong internal desire for growth, but the external environment must support this. Otherwise, these internal motivators will be thwarted. Rather than assuming, as the behaviorist approaches do, that people only respond to external reinforcements, SDT focuses on what human beings need and want to allow them to flourish.

SDT suggests that these needs fall into three categories: competence, relatedness, and autonomy (figure 3.3). Competence—or what is sometimes called mastery—means being effective in dealing with the external environment. Think of pulling off a difficult deal, learning how to dance the tango, or filing a tax return. It's about a sense of being able to do things in the world. Relatedness involves social connection and the universal desire to interact with and be involved with family, friends, and others. It can also manifest itself as a desire for higher purpose, or "making a difference." And finally, autonomy is the innate need to feel in command of one's life and to be doing that which is meaningful and in harmony with one's values. Contrast the unhappiness you experience when you are forced to do something

Figure 3.3: Elements of Self-Determination Theory

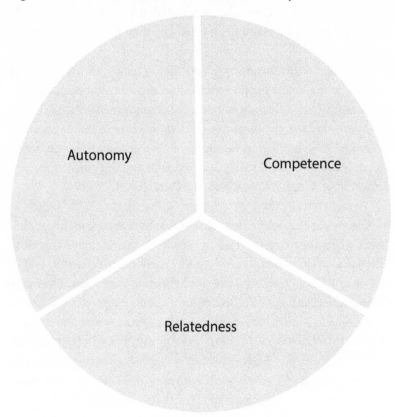

you don't want to do (or worse, that is contrary to your principles) with your feelings of joy when you are engaged in your favorite hobby or leading an important project at work.

Tasks that implicate one or more of these innate human needs will generally be intrinsically motivated. In other words, people do them for their own sake. Some examples are obvious: Think of any hobby you enjoy, creative activities like writing or drawing that give you pleasure or a sense of achievement, or the delight of attending a dinner party with friends or solving a difficult crossword puzzle. Other examples may not be as obvious, but they are no less intrinsically motivated. Think of the pleasure of reflecting on how well you ran that last project, or how great that sales pitch went, or how proud you felt mastering a difficult grammatical rule in a new language.

It's important to recognize that intrinsic motivation can come into play in the workplace and other serious settings, and that behavior can be intrinsically motivated even though an extrinsic reward system is already in place (e.g., salary and promotion). The psychologist Mihaly Csikszentmihalyi famously found that people most commonly experienced the state of ultimate intrinsic motivation—what he called flow—in the workplace. This means that we can find intrinsic motivation anywhere. Activities that address people's needs for competence, autonomy, and relatedness are absorbing, interesting, and *fun*, regardless of where they are found.

Think back to Duolingo. Players progress through different levels of a language, creating a sense of competence. They can choose to compete against others on leaderboards or unlock special content such as learning Italian words for Christmas or flirting, giving them a sense of autonomy. And they can ask questions and engage in discussion about the language they're studying with the Duolingo community, answering their relatedness needs. Duolingo language learners are probably unaware of all the ways that the app responds to their core SDT needs. But the success of the app speaks to how effectively von Ahn and his colleagues have marshaled these intrinsic motivators.

Bear in mind that these motivators will manifest differently in each individual. Some players will be put off by competition and find this acutely demotivating. This is why the designers of Duolingo allow players to elect to play this part of the language learning system—you can choose to compete or not, and it makes no difference to other parts of your language learning. Smart game designers realized they had to provide a range of different hooks for different sorts of players.

Popular video games often offer both player-vs.-player (PvP) and player-vs.-environment (PvE) challenges to address the two forms of competence. As one might expect, there are gender and age patterns here, but they aren't absolute. Both of the authors play World of

Warcraft (having returned to the game during the COVID-19 crisis). One of us loves nothing more than to sit in a secluded spot outside a major city and ambush passing players from the other side. The other puts much of his energy into bloodlessly accumulating a huge fortune in the game's auction house. To each his own.

Games are perfect illustrations of the lessons of SDT. Why do people play? As we've already said, no one forces them to. Even a simple game like Sudoku activates intrinsic needs for autonomy (which puzzle I solve and how I solve it is entirely up to me), competence (I figured it out!), and relatedness (I can share the achievement with my friends). In the same way, gamification uses the three intrinsic motivators to generate powerful results. Leveling up and accumulating points are markers of competence or mastery. Giving players choices and a range of experiences as they progress feeds their desire for autonomy and agency. Social interactions such as Facebook sharing or badges you can display to friends respond to the human need for relatedness.

Although games are fun in and of themselves, they are not just about intrinsic motivation and can also involve extrinsic motivators. If you like first-person shooter games and spend three blissful hours playing Call of Duty: Modern Warfare on your Xbox One, chances are you'll describe the experience as intrinsically rewarding. But if you play it to beat your best friend's high score, or to win the prize in a tournament, or because your professor assigned it as homework, you might say something different. The latter examples involve extrinsic motivation, and each of them is really powerful as a motivating force. The important lesson is that you can use both intrinsic and extrinsic motivation, and as the designer of a gamified system you'll have a series of choices about which motivational levers to pull, and how to do so.

This leads us to another important lesson: Pay careful attention to your proposed users. Consider three frequent fliers who have United Airlines Premier Elite status. Juan is proud of being in such an exclusive club—he loves the feeling of checking in on a red carpet so he doesn't have to queue with the economy passengers. Alice is just happy to have no luggage fees, and she loves that she can redeem miles for free trips. But all Esther cares about is access to the private airport lounges, where she can relax during those long layovers on business trips. Juan's craving for status is real, but it doesn't make that a good motivator for Alice or Esther. Recognize that each is motivated in different ways, and that any effective gamified system should recognize this.

In the next section we will generate some lessons for how you can start creating your own gamified processes. But let us give a few high-level warnings before we dive into the specifics of motivation:

- Don't oversimplify the ways that game elements or gamified systems can produce motivational responses.
- Don't assume one thing will work for all users.
- And don't overgeneralize about how people respond to certain stimuli.

Gamification is not just reward design. That sort of thinking is what led programming book author and game developer Kathy Sierra to label gamification "the high-fructose corn syrup of motivation." She has a point. Many gamified sites and gamification platforms seem to assume that a single virtual reward—points, say, or a badge—will be inherently compelling for all users. It probably won't be. It might be a pale substitute for what people really want. Or as we describe in the next section, it might actually kill intrinsic motivation. Good gamification depends on focus on building authentic engagement, and thinking about the motivations of many different types of users.

There are no shortcuts.

Lessons for Gamification

Now that we've described the basic framework for understanding motivation, what are the specific takeaways for successful gamification? The following five types of lessons are sometimes counterintuitive, but they are well supported by studies and real-world examples.

Don't Let Rewards Crowd Out Fun

Extrinsic rewards can be demotivating. Any gamification design has to take this into account. Sometimes giving people a bigger benefit to perform some activity will actually make them do it less, and do it worse. Alfie Kohn, the education reformer, published a book on this phenomenon in schools with the wonderful title *Punished by Rewards*, which documents multiple examples of how giving kids extrinsic rewards made their learning *worse* over time. Psychologists generally refer to this as the "crowding-out" problem, because extrinsic motivators tend to crowd out intrinsic ones. For tasks that are interesting or inherently valuable, intrinsic motivation dissipates when extrinsic rewards are tangible, expected, and contingent.

Consider how we learn to read. Many people find the pleasure of losing themselves in a book to be one of the true joys of life. It's one of the best examples of an intrinsically rewarding activity, at least when you read for the experience itself, not to achieve some other goal. But teaching kids to read can be an onerous task. Parents and teachers employ all manner of tricks to get them over the initial comprehension gap. Often these tricks fall on the more extrinsic side of the motivation continuum. It turns out that if you give kids tangible rewards like gold stars for doing well at reading—or, worse, if you give them money—they will improve up to a certain point and then stop. The initial tangible, expected, and contingent reward initially motivates the kids, but its effectiveness plateaus dramatically. The effect is so obvious that it's become known by the grade level at which the extrinsic motivation loses its power: It's called the Fourth Grade Slump.

The crowding-out effect may sound counterintuitive, but when you think about it, there are good reasons for it. Paying a person to do something implies it's not inherently enjoyable, rewarding, or important. (Consider why we call salary "compensation.") It suggests the task is only worth doing to the minimal extent necessary to get the reward. Before long, people begin to take the reward for granted. When the reward is expected, our mental arithmetic sees it as a kind of sunk benefit, providing increasingly little pleasure when it actually arrives. The task no longer seems intrinsically worthwhile, and the extrinsic rewards become increasingly poor substitutes.

Many research studies confirm that the crowding-out effect is real. Whether it's American children drawing pictures, Swiss citizens engaged in volunteer work, or Israeli parents showing up on time at day care, adding extrinsic rewards (or punishments) to intrinsically motivated tasks has been demonstrated to produce less effort and poorer-quality work. Moreover, the nature of the reward doesn't seem to matter. Virtually every type of expected reward and punishment that is contingent on performance will have a negative effect over time.

The lesson for gamification is simple: Don't mindlessly attach extrinsic motivators to activities that can be motivated intrinsically. Think back to the Microsoft Language Quality Game from Level 1. The reason the company didn't pay the participants for each dialog box error they found, or even award a prize to the best individual or region, isn't that it wanted to save money. The fact that Ross Smith's group substantially improved the quality of language localization at minimal cost was a positive feature but not the rationale for their approach. Money would have gotten in the way. The competition wasn't *work*; it was a fun challenge and a way to help the company produce better products. That's what made it so successful.

Recognize That Boring Can Be Engaging

We may seem like we're contradicting ourselves, but extrinsic motivation is not *always* bad. Studies have found it has a positive outcome on performance when the user is engaged in an *otherwise amotivated task*. In other words, extrinsic motivation helps people enjoy boring activities. Unlike the situation in which the task can be intrinsically motivated—like reading a novel—extrinsic rewards can encourage positive behavior and outcomes when a person is dealing with dull, repetitive, or tedious activities. And we all know that everyone runs into those at some point.

When should you use an extrinsic motivator? Think of the many tasks that are dull and will never be enjoyable. Imagine you are trying to motivate people to do their taxes or financial planning, take out the trash, or submit to an unpleasant but medically advisable colonoscopy. You may have to use extrinsic rewards and punishments to motivate people to change their preferred behavior—not to do it. What if you're trying to do something like make math more fun for middle-schoolers, nudge people to go to the gym, or encourage bank clients to understand the risks and rewards of financial products? In such cases, you may be able to apply intrinsic motivators, but extrinsic mechanisms may be necessary as a fallback.

Liveops is a call-center outsourcing provider. Using a software platform, it has created a low-cost, high-quality virtual workforce of 20,000 US-based call agents who answer or make calls part time from home. It has successfully won business by offering a better customer experience at comparable prices. A key asset for Liveops is its ability to offer unemployed and underemployed Americans, including those with significant time limitations such as stay-at-home mothers, gainful employment and online skills development. Call-center work can be the epitome of drudgery, but many Liveops agents describe their work in glowing terms.

Given its focus on creating positive experiences for its agents, Liveops is a natural candidate for gamification. Indeed, the company has embraced gamification as a way to improve motivation. By adding relatively simple game elements—such as leaderboards and points—Liveops generated significant results. Onboarding time went down from 160 hours to 14 hours, and agents who opted in to gamified processes outperformed their peers by 23% in average call handle time, according to the 2018 TalentLMS Gamification at Work survey. Customer satisfaction also rose by 9%. The emphasis of Liveops's gamification efforts is on learning and development rather than competition. Agents who level up or earn badges get the message that they are moving upward toward mastery of valuable skills.

There are numerous ways that you can use game mechanics to encourage certain types of behavior in tasks that can't be intrinsically motivated. A good example is in the traditional arena of marketing. Here, the experience of doing relatively mundane tasks with the promise of recognition or rewards to follow has been shown to be well received by consumers. Rewards programs give purchasers points, tiers, and other psychological rewards in exchange for behaviors desired by program creators—usually the purchase of more product, or engaging with it in some way—and this has been shown to be an effective motivator of favorable activity.

The lesson for gamification: Extrinsic reward systems work for activities that are not intrinsically engaging.

Tune Your Feedback

Feedback is trendy these days. Businesses and governments can now collect and display data to users in real time, and they are deriving significant value in doing so. Police have shown a marked decrease in speeding by displaying the driver's speed on a roadside radar detector. Drivers of hybrid vehicles use less gas when they are shown how accelerating and braking affects their mileage per gallon. Homeowners turn their thermostats down when given real-time feedback on what happens when they turn them up. Designed well, feedback loops push users toward desired behaviors.

Feedback in a gamified system can be the linchpin of effective motivation, and it doesn't have to be complicated. Duolingo specializes in simple feedback loops: If you stop logging in to learn your language, not only does Duo, the green owl, send you reminder notifications, but you lose your winning streak. More complicated loops include diminishing strength bars to show that your language retention is probably waning, to encourage you to go back and revisit old lessons.

You will need to adopt some similar techniques if you are going to get feedback right. Here are three important lessons about feedback:

1. Unexpected, informational feedback increases autonomy and self-reported intrinsic motivation. This has some concrete pay-offs. It means that people enjoy being surprised by achievements and rewards that they didn't anticipate. Unlike the demotivating grind of contingent, expected rewards—for example, when you know that if you tweet 100 times about a product you will get a "You Tweeted 100 Times About Our Product" badge—getting an unexpected badge or trophy stimulates positive feelings in the user. Players get a dopamine surge when it happens, a little like hitting a jackpot on a slot machine. This mechanism is called a "variable reward schedule," and it's a well-established design pattern in game development that you can use in gamification projects.

2. Users like to get reinforcement about how they are doing. Informational feedback about progress toward a goal will typically engage a player and may motivate them to complete the other steps necessary to fulfill the task. So think of creating a gamified mechanic that rewards the player with some feedback: "You've completed three out of the five steps necessary to unlock the AWESOME JOB level." Or consider providing a graph of the player's performance against specific metrics. This is also something game designers have known for a long time. Video games are veritable feedback fests, filled with scoreboards, flashing colors, musical fanfare, and more, whenever something important happens, like clearing a level in Candy Crush Saga.

3. Users will regulate their own behavior based on which metrics are provided to them. If you provide feedback loops about customer satisfaction but not about sales figures, your sales team will begin to care more about customer satisfaction than monthly sales. If you give them leaderboards about sales figures, guess what your team is going to focus on? Used wisely, this is a powerful tool in any gamified system—but bear in mind that all of the lessons and rules previously discussed still apply. If you create a feedback loop that works as an extrinsic motivator, you should expect that this may crowd out any intrinsic sense of satisfaction that the user might otherwise have experienced.

The lesson for gamification: Feedback loops regulate behavior in the direction of the feedback, and providing metrics for success will motivate the player in that direction.

Work Across the Motivational Continuum

Not all extrinsic motivation is experienced as completely outside the person's self. Imagine three students—Anna, Bella, and Celia— slogging their way through some statistics homework. Anna does it because she knows her parents will punish her if she doesn't do it; Bella does it because she is an A-type personality and hates to fail even more than she hates math; and Celia does it because she needs to pass math so she can fulfill her dream of becoming an economist. Anna experiences the motivation unhappily as external to herself—she will be punished if she doesn't do it—whereas Bella and Celia experience the motivation as extrinsic, but somehow more meaningful.

Students like Bella and Celia have taken the extrinsic motivation and internalized it within their set of values and sense of self. Deci and Ryan suggest that extrinsic motivation operates on a sort of continuum outside the person's sense of self through a number of stages that are more and more integrated into the person's internal experience. Any task that a person wouldn't do except for motivations like rewards or punishments—Anna's experience—is generally perceived as external. Tasks that are motivated by ego like Bella's are marginally internalized—"I must do well at school"—and are called "introjected," because it's as if the extrinsic motivation is being inserted into the person. Tasks that people like Celia see as important to their future or to their values become part of them, and they are labeled as "integrated" or "identified."

A perfect example can be seen in online role-playing games like World of Warcraft, which encourages the formation of tight-knit groups called guilds that provide a system of mutual support for players. When players are part of the group, they cheerfully perform tasks that are dull—collecting materials or slaying low-level monsters repeatedly to reach reputation thresholds—which they'd never do without the group. It's not that the task changes; it's that the user's need for relatedness—"my guild members need me"—dramatically changes the perceived nature of the motivation. The motivation becomes internalized as the player recognizes the value of the task to the guild.

The lesson here for any gamification design is significant: It is possible to design extrinsic motivators that become introjected, internalized, or integrated into the user's sense of self, and so become more compelling to the user. Points and leaderboards are a good example: These gamification mechanisms can be seen as generating introjected behavior regulators because they appeal to a user's ego by allowing them to brag about their standing. Another example: Social gaming mechanisms allow users to become part of a larger community, which makes them care more about the gamification mechanism than they otherwise would. The motivator that was previously experienced as external to the user will begin to form part of the internal system of motivation, as the meaning of their community takes on greater value to them.

Don't Be Evil

Just because you can motivate someone to do something doesn't mean you should. One of our colleagues was asked to advise a large call-center operator on using game mechanics to increase productivity. He concluded that doing so would take an already awful work environment for the call-center agents and make it even worse. The gamification would be a tool for monitoring and dehumanizing the workers, not genuinely rewarding them. So, he turned the job down.

Gamification can motivate people to undertake activities that they otherwise wouldn't do. If that means hitting the gym regularly or having a more enjoyable engagement with a brand, it's a good thing. If it means your users are gambling away their paychecks at a casino or are being manipulated into taking valueless badges when they really wanted cash, it's troublesome. The best example of this is Uber. As we will explore in Level 6, Uber has attracted huge consumer and driver backlash for its gamified elements that push drivers to work harder, often past the limits of human endurance.

In short, it's dangerous to see gamification as a covert tool to squeeze more out of customers, employees, or other groups. Instead, look at it as a means to produce authentic happiness and to help people flourish while achieving your own goals at the same time.

Level 4

The Gamification Toolkit
Game Elements

[I asked my three-year-old daughter what she was made of.]
She paused to consider. She looked down at her hands,
turning them over, and studying them. And then, brightly,
she announced: "I'm made of skin!"
—Jesse Schell, *The Art of Game Design*

Now that you have earned your way to Level 4, you know how to think about your problem in gamification terms, you understand how to motivate your users, and you have seen how to implement a basic gamification system. It's time to level up to some more advanced features of game thinking so that you can deliver the most compelling implementation. We'll ask the following questions:

- *What are points, badges, and leaderboards (PBLs), and why are they so common in gamification?*
- *What are game elements, and how can you apply them?*

Back in the early days of gamification—2010—USA Network built a gamified website around its successful TV program *Psych*. Club Psych offered users an array of challenges, such as watching a video, answering trivia questions, and joining the show's fan club (figure 4.1). A mystery game called Hashtag Killer allowed players to simulate interactions with the show's characters over Twitter and Facebook. The mobile version, called Psych Vision, let fans unlock

Figure 4.1: Club Psych's Original Gamified Website

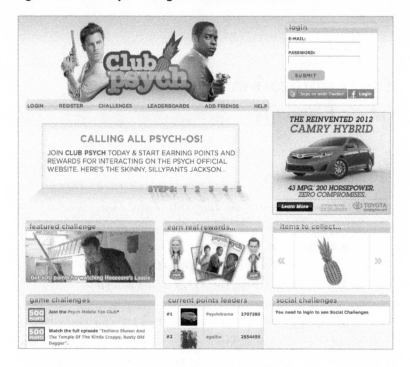

prizes and chat with each other while watching the show on TV. All of these actions earned the user points that could be redeemed for virtual goods or physical merchandise, including posters signed by the show's cast. Items were added and removed to stimulate continued interest.

The most obvious surface-level gamification features of Club Psych were PBLs. Players accumulated points for undertaking challenges and could redeem them for rewards. A leaderboard allowed players to compare themselves with other players.

Club Psych employed PBLs effectively: After the introduction of the gamified site, overall traffic on the USA Network site increased 30%, online merchandise sales increased nearly 50%, and page views for the official *Psych* website increased 130%. Club Psych's users were undoubtedly more engaged than the average couch potato. And they shared *Psych* content hundreds of thousands of times on Facebook, reaching 40 million Facebook users at its peak. Considering that *Psych* had only about 4.5 million regular viewers, that's a tremendous amount of publicity for the show. Hashtag Killer was even nominated for an Emmy Award.

It's not surprising that in 2010, Club Psych would focus on PBLs to effectively employ gamification—back then, PBLs were pretty much the only thing people thought of when they considered gamifying their processes. We've come a long way since.

PBLs still have their place, but that doesn't mean effective gamification is just about adding them to your business process and calling it a day. Although PBLs are incredibly common in gamification, they are not the whole story, especially today. Sometimes, they can even be damaging to what you want to do. Jesse Schell, the noted games designer and Carnegie Mellon University professor, tells the story about his daughter's idea that she's made of skin to convey that a surface-level understanding of the human body is fine for a three-year-old, but it's not so great if you're a physician. Hopefully your internist knows you're not made of skin.

The same is true of gamification. You will learn that gamification is more than skin-deep elements like PBLs. In the course of this chapter, we'll work deeper into the body of gamification to examine the muscles, skeleton, and large organs that you will be able to use to develop compelling gamification projects.

The PBL Triad

In our research, we've examined hundreds of gamification implementations. Many of these systems, if not the majority of them, start with the same three elements: points, badges, and leaderboards. PBLs are so common within gamification that they are often described as though they *are* gamification. They're not, but they are a good place to start.

Used correctly, PBLs are powerful, practical, and relevant. They can also be used in significantly more sophisticated ways than one might imagine. Thus, they are the obvious place to start building your gamification toolkit. But they have important limitations. To build a successful gamification system, you need to understand their pros and cons.

Points

In a gamified process, points are used to encourage people to do things by tying the collection of points to desired activities. Think of frequent-flier loyalty programs: The airline wants you as a repeat customer, so it rewards you with redeemable points for each flight you take. The assumption underlying point systems is that people will fly more, buy more widgets, or recycle more in exchange for points. This is a simple approach that occasionally works to motivate those who like collecting things ("Look at how many points I just received!") or those who like competing against others ("No one else has one million points!").

But points can be used in many other ways, and a good designer of gamified systems will recognize that the humble point can serve many functions. We've identified six ways that points are used in gamification:

1. **Points keep score.** This is the typical use of points in gamification systems. Points tell the player how well they are doing. Someone who has earned 32,768 points has been playing longer or more successfully than someone with 24,813 points. Points can also demarcate levels. For example, content unlocking and badge reward processes—great game mechanics for many players—are often tied to points: "At 10,000 points you reach Platinum Flier Status, where you get a fancy new card and can check bags for free." In this case, points represent the true "play space" of a game because they define progress from the beginning of the game to its objectives.
2. **Points may determine the win state of a gamified process (assuming it has one).** Sometimes you will want to use points

to create a win condition, such as if you want to give away a prize.

3. **Points create a connection between progression in the game and extrinsic rewards.** Many gamified systems offer some real-world prizes for reaching certain levels or for redeeming virtual points: 1,000 points gets you a set of steak knives, and one million points gets you a round-trip ticket to Tahiti. This is common in many marketing and promotional devices.

4. **Points provide feedback.** Explicit and frequent feedback is a key element in most good game design, and points provide feedback quickly and easily. Points are among the most granular of feedback mechanisms. Each point gives the user a tiny bit of feedback—and a tiny hit of dopamine—telling them that they are doing well and progressing in the game.

5. **Points can be an external display of progress.** In a multi-player game, or in an environment in which members of the community or workplace can see each other's scores, points show others how you are doing. That can be significant as a marker of status, a powerful motivator.

6. **Points provide data for the game designer.** The points that users earn can easily be tracked and stored. This allows the designer to analyze important metrics about the system. For example, how fast are users progressing through the content? Do they seem to be falling off or stalling out at certain junctures?

By understanding the nature of points, you can use them in ways that meet the objectives of your gamified system. Do you want to encourage competition? Then use points as scores that all can see. Do you want your players to be hooked on feedback? Then use points to give them a sense of mastery and progression, without showing them how others are doing. And so on.

Bear in mind that points are limited. They are uniform, abstract, interchangeable, and, well, point-like. A point is just a point. Each additional point simply indicates a greater magnitude and nothing more. This is one reason why badges are often found in conjunction with point systems—badges give context and meaning to points.

Badges

Badges are a chunkier version of points. A badge is a visual representation of some achievement within the gamified process. (The terms "badges" and "achievements" are often used synonymously in gamification.) Some badges simply demarcate a certain level of points. Fitbit is a gamified system that allows people to use a wireless pedometer to track the number of miles they walk or run. Along with more complicated gamified elements, the system includes an array of badges (figure 4.2). Among other things, badges celebrate hitting walking milestones daily, on weekends, and five workdays in a row.

Other badges signify different kinds of activities. Today, Foursquare is a location-data company used behind the scenes by dozens of Fortune 100 companies. But it got into this game through its sophisticated gamification, in particular its amusing and effective badging system. The platform connected people with local businesses

Figure 4.2: Fitbit Badges

Rocket Boots

Great Barrier Reef

Accomplishment: You've walked 90,000 steps in one day.

Accomplishment: You've walked 1,600 miles since joining Fitbit.

by encouraging users to check in to a location with their cell phones—with numerous badges for all manner of "achievements." Users unlocked the Adventurer badge as soon as they checked into 10 places; and they received the Crunked badge for checking into four bars in one night. (No one said that badges need to be socially responsible.)

Researchers Judd Antin and Elizabeth Churchill suggest that a well-designed badge system has five motivational characteristics:

1. Badges can provide a goal for users to strive toward, which has been shown to have positive effects on motivation.
2. Badges provide guidance as to what is possible within the system and generate a kind of shorthand of what the system is supposed to do. This is an important feature for "onboarding," or getting the user engaged with the system.
3. Badges are a signal of what a user cares about and what he or she has performed. They are a kind of visual marker of a user's reputation, and users will often acquire badges to try to show others what they are capable of.
4. Badges operate as virtual status symbols and affirmations of the personal journey of the user through the gamification system.
5. Badges function as tribal markers. A user who has some of the same badges as other users will feel a sense of identity with that group, and a clever gamification design can connect the badges with a system of group identification.

One of the most important attributes of badges is their flexibility. Many different kinds of badges can be awarded for many different kinds of activities, and the range of badges is limited only by the imagination of the gamification designer and the needs of the business. This allows the gamified service to engage a more diverse group of users and to appeal to their interests in ways that a single point system cannot. Your friend may have a completely different set of badges than you, even though you're both playing the same game.

Nonetheless, both you and your friend can find your individual badges meaningful and interesting.

Badges can also serve a credentialing function. Many people have relied on the Good Housekeeping Seal of Approval. Since 1909, the seal has told consumers that the product in question passed tests by *Good Housekeeping* magazine. That means you don't have to trust the product; you just have to trust *Good Housekeeping.* The same is true for gold stars awarded to wines from prestigious shows, the *Motor Trend* Car of the Year award, or even the Academy Award for Best Picture. These are all types of badges, and one of the nice things about badges as credentials is that they are infinitely flexible. You can receive a badge for anything, from the silly to the serious. We have seen this in the development of badges as a foundation for new forms of online education and training—micro-credentialed badges are now found in numerous training scenarios, and even in colleges and universities. This isn't as crazy as it might first sound: when you think about it, a diploma from an elite university is a kind of badge that holds out the promise of a certain level of skill and achievement on the part of the diploma holder.

In internal gamification contexts, credentialing badges can be a way for your employees to demonstrate certain skills. Every large enterprise has extensive corporate training programs, and employees participate in more training outside the firm. Badge systems are useful in this context.

Leaderboards

Leaderboards are the final leg of the PBL triad, and perhaps the most troublesome. On the one hand, players often want to know where they stand relative to their peers. A leaderboard gives context to progression in a way that points or badges can't. If performance in the game matters, the leaderboard makes that performance public for all to see. In the right situation, leaderboards can be powerful motivators. Knowing that it's just a few more points to move up a slot or even to emerge on top can be a strong push for users.

On the other hand, leaderboards can be powerfully demotivating. If you see exactly how far you are behind the top players, it can cause you to check out and stop trying. Leaderboards can also reduce the richness of a game to a zero-sum struggle for supremacy, which inherently turns off some people and makes others behave in less desirable ways. Several studies have shown that introducing a leaderboard alone in a business environment will usually reduce performance rather than enhance it.

There are various ways to make leaderboards work for your gamified system. A leaderboard need not be a static scoreboard, and it need not track only one attribute. In gamification, leaderboards can track any feature or features the designer wants to emphasize. There's nothing wrong with multiple leaderboards measuring different things or leaderboards that aren't universal for all participants. Leaderboards can also be tied to social networks to provide more contextual information about how players are faring.

But be careful how you use leaderboards. Although some studies have shown leaderboards can provide useful performance assists in workplace settings, one randomized experiment involving salespeople placed on leaderboards showed problems could arise. Notably, women tended to perform *better* when leaderboards were removed from the workplace. And otherwise successful salespeople of all genders could become demotivated if their ranking was lower than they expected.

This means you have to be careful in how you design a leaderboard. Duolingo, the gamified language app, lets language learners opt in to compete on a leaderboard. If they do, they're placed in competition with 50 other players who are selected at random. In the course of the week, the players compete against each other to learn the most in their chosen language. At the end of the week, the top three are promoted to the next league, and (unless they're already in the bottom league) the bottom 10 are demoted.

For a range of reasons, this is a smart design. It is an opt-in process, so only people who like this sort of thing will compete. It motivates the most competitive learners to strive against equally competitive players, and over time people find their own levels. Each week you are competing against different players, so there is a kind of anonymity to your competition: you're trying to beat FinnishLearner76 this week, but you won't constantly be beaten by them each week. And it allows the players to use the leaderboard for their own reasons: Some just want to stay in the Obsidian League, some want to advance each week, and some will use the threat of demotion to do another two or three classes this week so that they stay in the Gold League.

As you can see, leaderboards can push a lot of motivational buttons.

PBLs as a Starting Point

The PBL triad forms a useful starting point for gamification efforts. In our early gamification courses for Wharton MBA students, almost every student team incorporated PBLs into their gamification design, despite our admonitions to consider alternatives. There's just something comfortable about these components, and they make sense in a lot of projects. Related to this, turnkey gamification products almost always incorporate these three elements as standard features. It's therefore easy to implement these three approaches using off-the-shelf products. And PBLs link gamification to well-known enterprise features like loyalty programs, reputation systems, and employee competitions.

As valuable as they are, relying just on PBLs can get you into trouble. PBLs aren't right for every project, and they are not the only features that you can deploy in a gamified system. If you want to extract the maximum value from gamification, you'll want to move beyond PBLs. This is where we head next, where we start to think a little more about what makes a game work.

Braving the Elements

We've already seen a number of gamification features that are not PBLs, in examples like the teams in the Language Quality Game, or the feedback loops in Duolingo. It turns out that PBLs are special cases of what we will call "game elements"—that is, specific characteristics of games that you can apply in gamification.

To build a house, you need to understand small-scale components such as hammers and nails and 2 × 4s; midlevel concepts such as framing, plumbing, and blueprints; and high-level abstractions such as master bathrooms, structural engineering, movement flow, and aesthetics. Each of those is an element of house construction. The sum total of the elements and the ways they are put together is the house itself. Architects and builders go from a vacant lot to a finished house using such elements. Project managers and designers in charge of gamification understand games in a similar way and can use this understanding to build, pull apart, and rebuild their projects.

There are three categories of game elements that are relevant to gamification: dynamics, mechanics, and components. They are organized from the most abstract to the least. Each mechanic is tied to one or more dynamics, and each component is tied to one or more higher-level elements.

Dynamics

At the highest level of abstraction are dynamics. The most important game dynamics are the following:

1. Constraints (limitations or forced trade-offs)
2. Emotions (curiosity, competitiveness, frustration, happiness, etc.)
3. Narrative (a consistent, ongoing storyline)
4. Progression (the player's growth and development)
5. Relationships (social interactions generating feelings of camaraderie, status, altruism, etc.)

Dynamics are the big-picture aspects of the gamified system that you have to consider and manage but that you can never directly place into the game. Analogies in the management world would be employee development, creating an innovation culture, or pretty much any other large-scale objective you'll find in an airport book on business. The dynamics in Club Psych included high-level features like the way that the prizes relate to the narrative in the television series (for example, bobblehead dolls of the actors and a recurring appearance of a pineapple) or the relationships formed when users are able to comment on the latest episode.

There's an important point here. Good leaders create desired dynamics in their organizations. They rarely, if ever, have the opportunity to sit outside the organization and design it from scratch. Rather, they have to push an existing institution in the right direction through hiring and promotion, management practices, and leading by example. When creating a gamified system, on the other hand, you can play God. You're the designer. The way to think outside the box in gamification is to build a better box.

Mechanics

Mechanics are the basic processes that drive the action forward and generate player engagement. We can identify 10 important game mechanics:

1. Challenges (puzzles or other tasks that require effort to solve)
2. Chance (elements of randomness)
3. Competition (one player or group wins, and the other loses)
4. Cooperation (players work together to achieve a shared goal)
5. Feedback (information about how the player is doing)
6. Resource acquisition (obtaining useful or collectible items)
7. Rewards (benefits for some action or achievement)
8. Transactions (trading between players, directly or through intermediaries)
9. Turns (sequential participation by alternating players)
10. Win states (objectives that make one player or group the winner—draw and loss states are related concepts)

Each mechanic is a way of achieving one or more of the dynamics described. An award that pops up without warning (Mechanic 2—Chance) may stimulate players' sense of fun and curiosity (Dynamic 2—Emotions). It may also be a way of getting new participants hooked or keeping experienced players involved (Dynamic 4—Progression). In Club Psych, mechanics involved social challenges, like watching preview clips with your friends, and rewards that ranged from virtual goods to rare merchandise.

Components

Components are more specific forms mechanics or dynamics can take. In the first edition of this book, we identified the following 15 important game components:

1. Achievements (defined objectives)
2. Avatars (visual representations of a player's character)
3. Badges (visual representations of achievements)
4. Boss fights (especially hard challenges at the culmination of a level)
5. Collections (sets of items or badges to accumulate)
6. Combat (a defined battle, typically short-lived)
7. Content unlocking (aspects available only when players reach objectives)
8. Gifting (opportunities to share resources with others)
9. Leaderboards (visual displays of player progression and achievement)
10. Levels (defined steps in player progression)
11. Points (numerical representations of game progression)
12. Quests (predefined challenges with objectives and rewards)
13. Social graphs (representation of players' social network within the game)
14. Teams (defined groups of players working together for a common goal)

15. Virtual goods (game assets with perceived or real-money value)

Our framework and these components were studied and validated in a 2019 study by researchers at the University of Limerick in Ireland. They confirmed that all of the above elements were found in gamified systems. The most used elements were points (found in 79% of gamified systems) and achievements (78.4%); while the least used were boss fights (17.5% of the time) and gifting (13.8%).

The researchers also noted the presence of other components that we had not initially identified but that were found in 30% or more of newer gamified systems:

16. Infinite gameplay (allowing constant play)
17. Progression bar (a numeric or visual representation of progress toward completing a mission)
18. Search and discovery (a number of distinct paths toward mission completion)
19. Time constraints (racing against the clock)
20. Tangible rewards (in game progress converted into currency, products, or services)
21. Negative scoring

Just as each mechanic ties to one or more dynamics, each component ties to one or more higher-level elements. Gamified systems such as Club Psych often use points and badges extensively to connect player actions to the higher-level mechanics and dynamics. Players working on puzzles that relate to a current episode could earn points, thus answering challenges, receiving feedback, moving closer to rewards, and connecting to the narrative context of the television series. Or if they reached high-enough levels, they could collect limited-availability badges that were themed from the series (resource acquisition, rewards, narrative, progression, constraints).

Integration

We've given you a lot of information about game elements in fairly general terms. It may not all feel coherent right away. We've provided quick sketches of different sorts of game elements so that you understand that there are lots of features you can use, and so that you have some ideas to try out. For those wanting to do a deeper dive into game elements, we've created a companion ebook called *The Gamification Toolkit*, which elaborates on each of them.

In the next level, we take the basics of game elements and show you how to use the design process to apply these elements. But you should now have a sense that all of the game elements exist in a hierarchy, as shown in figure 4.3.

Figure 4.3: The Game Element Hierarchy

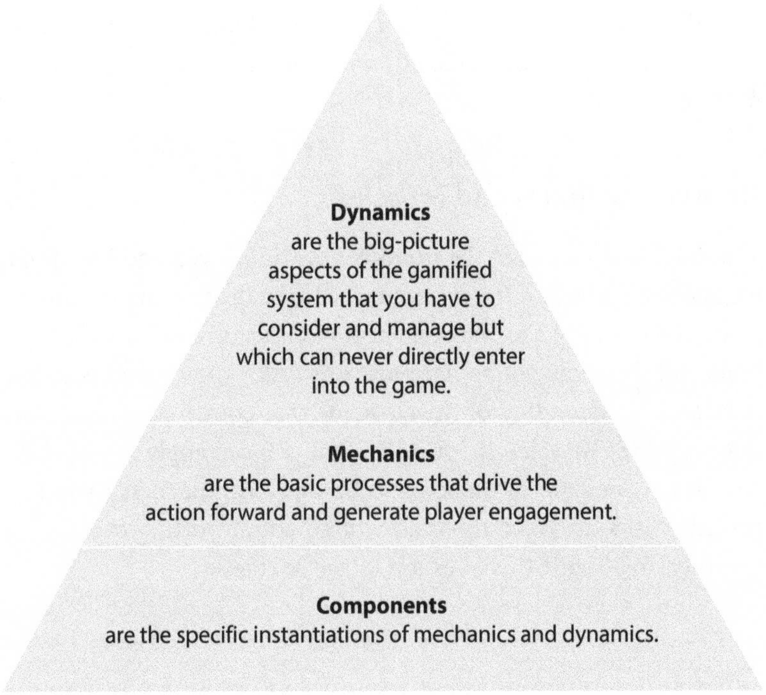

Dynamics
are the big-picture
aspects of the gamified
system that you have to
consider and manage but
which can never directly enter
into the game.

Mechanics
are the basic processes that drive the
action forward and generate player engagement.

Components
are the specific instantiations of mechanics and dynamics.

Putting all these elements together is the central task of gamification design, and having knowledge of these game elements will make your gamification project compelling. Bear in mind, though, that no gamification project will include all of these elements. In fact, it's unlikely you would ever utilize all the items within any one category. However, if you haven't considered a large set of possible options at some stage of your design process, your gamification project will suffer. As we move up to the next level, you'll see how to integrate these elements into the gamification design process.

One final caveat: Having a list of elements is necessary but by no means sufficient. Creating a successful new service is always harder than deconstructing an existing one. In particular, building an engaging gamified service takes more than checking off the right boxes. You need to ensure that the elements match the particular demands of your situation.

And execution matters a lot! When they first launched, Facebook, Friendster, and MySpace were social networking sites with similar basic capabilities. One made billions. The other two are historical footnotes.

Beyond the Bones and Muscles

When we first looked at the examples of Club Psych and Duolingo, we saw the surface of the system but not the organs that lay underneath the skin. PBLs form the most obvious features of gamified systems, but they may not be right for your task. And though you now have an understanding of the elements that constitute games—the bones and the muscles, if you will—that you can apply to your process, it may be hard to understand how you can harness them in a meaningful way. How, then, do you go about putting everything together? We tackle this question in the next level.

Game Changer
Six Steps to Gamification

> *Games are the most elevated form of investigation.*
> —Albert Einstein

This is where we bring all of our learning together. We now have all the building blocks to make gamification work. At Level 5, we see how to make it happen, by looking at the following:

- *Gamification as a design process*
- *Six steps to implement gamification effectively*
- *Techniques to apply high-level concepts to specific projects*

Now that you know the essential concepts of gamification and game thinking, it's time to use them. This has to be done in a thoughtful way. If your process boils down to brainstorming what might be fun for your players and picking the game elements that seem to work, there's a good chance you'll fail. Whether you are going to create, plan, execute, and assess a gamification project yourself or leave the implementation to outside service providers, you're going to need a process to make the project work.

Gamification requires a fusion of art and science. On the one hand, it involves emotional concepts such as fun, play, and user experiences. On the other hand, it's about engineering measurable and sustainable systems to serve concrete business objectives. Creative types tend to focus on the experience and give short shrift to metrics.

The quants and MBAs, however, can lose sight of the big picture amid their spreadsheets.

Fortunately, there's a discipline that bridges this gap: It's called design. A good design process melds creativity and structure to match people's needs with technical feasibility and business realities. Entire books have been written on design thinking in business. Here we offer a design framework that is customized for developing gamified systems.

Gamification is best implemented in six steps, each of which starts—like the word "design"—with the letter *D*:

1. DEFINE business objectives.
2. DELINEATE target behaviors.
3. DESCRIBE your players.
4. DEVISE activity cycles.
5. DON'T forget the fun!
6. DEPLOY the appropriate tools.

You will see that only in the last step do we talk about gamification components like leaderboards and badges. That's deliberate. The mechanisms of gamification look really easy, especially today with so many plug-and-play tools readily available. If anything, they are too easy. The fact that you can add points to your website with a few lines of code and white-label software-as-a-service doesn't mean that you should. Designing how to map the available techniques onto your particular situation is what's difficult, which is why we spend the first five steps focusing on these issues.

1. Define Your Business Objectives

You started to do this in Level 1, but it's time to make things absolutely concrete. For effective gamification, it's critical to have a well-developed understanding of your goals. That might sound obvious, but it's easily overlooked. We're not talking here about your overall organizational mission, whether expressed in terms of profitability, shareholder value, mission statement, or otherwise. We mean the specific performance goals for your gamified system, such as increasing customer retention, building brand loyalty, or improving employee productivity. If you don't start with this step, your gamification project may get off the ground but will probably fail eventually.

DevHub is a small business website-building tool that was looking to increase engagement using gamification. DevHub's founders figured that game elements could overcome the fatigue that kept most users from implementing all the functions the site offered. They added experience points, levels, and virtual currency that could be redeemed for additional content and features. Next, they relaunched DevHub's website-building service as an empire-building game, complete with a stable of cartoon characters called Devatars that appeared on users' sites when they completed tasks. The percentage of users completing site-building activities increased eightfold. Even better, virtual goods became a new revenue stream, representing almost 30% of DevHub's revenues after the relaunch.

A great gamification success story, right? Wrong.

At that point, DevHub had attracted only about 10,000 active users. The numbers may have looked good on a percentage basis, but the reality was that the virtual goods brought in only about 40 cents per user per month. Enticing users to complete tasks didn't help with DevHub's real problem: attracting large numbers of users and monetizing their actions. It may have even hurt, by alienating potential customers who found the space empire game silly. DevHub had to lay off staff and search for a new business model. (It eventually made a successful pivot into a white-label service for digital marketing.)

The lesson from DevHub is that gamification, even when effective, can produce results that don't necessarily help. To avoid this pitfall, your first step is to make a list of all potential objectives (figure 5.1). Make each goal as precise as possible, but the initial list can be expansive because you'll winnow it down. Perhaps you want to attract high school dropouts from low-income communities to use

Figure 5.1: The Objective Definition Process

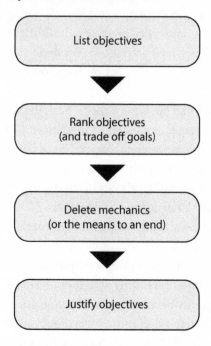

your personal finance educational tool, or perhaps you want your employees to suggest out-of-the-box ideas for new business opportunities. Then rank the list in terms of importance. You may need to trade off lesser goals for more significant ones, at least initially.

Now, go through your list and cross off anything that is a means rather than an end. In other words, it's really only a stepping-stone to a more important goal. Getting users to accumulate points and badges isn't a reason to implement a gamified system; it's something that happens within one. Having large numbers of players visit your website is only an end if it's directly valuable to you; otherwise it might generate support costs without concomitant revenues. A good test is whether you would be satisfied if something you listed were the only result from your gamification project. As a final check, add another column and, next to each objective, explain how it would benefit your organization.

As you work through your design and development process, keep coming back to this goal list. Even if your priorities change, it will keep you grounded and focused on what really matters.

2. Delineate Your Target Behaviors

Once you've identified why you're gamifying, focus on what you want your players to do and how you'll measure them. Behaviors and metrics are best considered together. Target behaviors should be concrete and specific. For example:

- Sign up for an account on your website.
- Post a comment on a discussion board.
- Exercise for at least 30 minutes.
- Share information about your service on Twitter.
- Complete the sexual harassment training module.
- Comment or vote on suggestions by others.
- Submit a 300-word summary of this week's reading for class.
- Visit your restaurant.

The behaviors you are looking for should promote the ultimate objectives you previously defined, though the relationship may be indirect. For example, getting users to spend more time on your site or talk about your products on Facebook doesn't translate immediately to revenue, but it may still be desirable.

Come up with as many possible behaviors as you can. You don't want the system to be too complex or confusing, but you want to give users a range of options and activities to pursue based on their preferences.

Once you've listed all the desired behaviors, develop your metrics for success. These are the ways you translate behaviors into quantifiable results. Gamification runs on software algorithms. Behind the scenes, it translates activities into numbers and uses those numbers to generate feedback. The numbers may or may not be transparent to players. They might see fireworks and an announcement that they've reached the "grand poobah" level or unlocked the "hungry hippo" achievement. In designing the system, however, you need to decide precisely what those mean.

As we discussed in Level 4, points are an easy way to quantify and measure any kind of progress. Whether or not your gamified system will present the user with points, you'll probably use them internally to define the relative values of behaviors in your design process. The value of the points should correspond to your best estimate of the relative value of the activities to your organization. For example, you may decide that reading a discussion post is worth 1 point, whereas commenting on it is worth 5 points, and posting is worth 10. You'll quite likely find that you need to tweak these point values once you start testing your system. Do the best you can at the outset, and be prepared to revise.

"Win states" form a second kind of success metric. Of course, everyone likes to win, and so it seems like a no-brainer to include some kind of "win" for your users. However, from a design standpoint, winning is problematic. It means that some players haven't won, and this may turn them off. And for those who do win, it means that the game, or that part of the game, is over. That's not good if your goal is to get them to keep coming back. Remember, your goal isn't to sell a game; it's to use game elements to achieve some organizational objective. You can get around these limitations to some degree by creating localized or temporal win states. Perhaps every week there's a new contest, or "winning" just means an achievement. Foursquare added levels to many of its badges when it realized its single state badges created an all-or-nothing dynamic rather than encouraging continued progression.

Analytics are the algorithms and data used to measure key performance indicators for your gamified system. Every online activity generates an event that can be tracked and measured. E-commerce and social games companies have become adept at learning how to aggregate data from large numbers of user transactions to measure the success of their services. Common analytics include the ratio of daily to monthly active users (an indication of how often users return), "virality" (how likely users are to refer their friends to the service), and the total volume of points awarded or virtual goods purchased. The right things to measure will depend on your context; an enterprise gamification project will likely involve analytics that are different from those of a marketing project, for example. Don't forget to identify whether existing monitoring systems within your organization are tracking the same behaviors.

3. Describe Your Players

There will be real people using your system. Who are they? What is their relationship to you? Employees, for example, aren't in the same situation as customers. How much does their relationship with you involve others?

What might motivate your players? That question probably won't have an easy answer, but put yourself in their shoes and identify as many possible motivations as you can. The discussion of intrinsic and extrinsic motivation at Level 3 should give you a good foundation for deciding which motivators can most effectively be addressed through your gamified system. Don't forget to think about what demotivates your players. In other words, what makes them less likely to complete a relevant task: Is it volition (a perceived lack of desire) or faculty (a perceived lack of capability)? The former calls for an engagement-oriented approach, while the latter calls for progression systems that gently walk the player up the difficulty curve.

Remember that not all users are the same. You'll want to segment your players so that your system is appropriate for more than one subgroup. Segmentation is a common practice in marketing and human resources. It's even more important here. Because games and gamified systems typically offer choices to the player, you don't need to choose a single segment to target. There are World of Warcraft players who do nothing but engage in player-to-player combat and others who spend all of their time exploring the world through solo quests. Similarly, gamified platforms can appeal in different ways to different groups.

Game designers have several models of player types that they use as starting points for segmentation. The best known was invented back in the late 1980s by games researcher Richard Bartle, who was studying early text-based multiplayer online games. It wasn't intended as a generalization for all games, let alone all user populations, but it's nonetheless a helpful heuristic for understanding why people play.

Bartle, whom we mentioned in the introduction, distinguished four player types: achievers, explorers, socializers, and killers. Achievers love the rush of leveling up or earning a badge; explorers want to find new content; socializers want to engage with friends; and killers want to impose their will on others, typically by vanquishing them. We all have elements of each of these archetypes. The proportions vary in different settings, and a player's primary motivation can shift over time. The best games and gamified systems have something to offer each category. Even the killers may be your friends if they function as elite "power users" or if they galvanize everyone else in a positive way.

Player modeling is a way to flesh out your segmentation to further guide your design process. Divide your player community into the categories that seem most appropriate. Perhaps you have a group of employees who are focused on proving their mettle to move up in the organization, a group that wants a sense of camaraderie, and a group that wants to feel that the work they do is producing something valuable.

Now, give each group the avatar of a typical player, with a name and a story. An avatar is just a virtual representation of someone. For example, Lucy is a graduate of an Ivy League school who came to work at your firm straight out of college and plans to eventually go back and get her MBA. Bob is a baby boomer, recently retired, who likes to play golf four days a week, and so on. Write a paragraph about each avatar. Where do they fit among the Bartle player types? What are their hopes and fears? Their talents? Their hobbies?

The more detailed the description of the avatars, the better. If the avatars don't ring true, if they don't reflect your likely audience, change them until they do. As you proceed in your gamification process, these character models will ground your design activities. It's easy to imagine how Lucy will respond to a particular quest mechanic. It's less easy to imagine how a nebulous Player A will respond to the same mechanic. And having a small number of representative avatars means that you can understand more easily how your system will appeal to different parts of your audience. It's easy to design for four representative avatars—Lucy, Bob, Layla, and Faraz—but it's hard to design for audience segments like "white, well-educated female players between 25 and 40," "blue-collar male players who don't like games," and so on.

The final dimension to consider is the player life cycle. Everyone starts as a novice, sometimes called a newbie or "noob" in game circles. Novices need hand-holding to learn the ropes. They may need reinforcement so that they can succeed or so that their friends are also involved. Once the novice becomes a regular, he or she needs novelty in order to stick with the activity. What was at first new and challenging is now effortless. Finally, the player becomes an expert. Experts need challenges that are hard enough to keep them engaged. They also tend to want explicit reinforcement of their status. All your players won't be at the same stage at the same time, although the longer your system runs, the more it will skew toward the experienced end. You must offer opportunities for players at all stages.

4. Devise Your Activity Cycles

Games always have a beginning and sometimes have an end, but along the way they operate through a series of loops and branching trees. In other words, the game isn't simply linear: *Step 1 → Step 2 → Step 3 → Completion.* There may be a leveling system that looks that way, but the overall gamification system behind the scenes isn't so simple. If it were, the system would just be a lockstep series of stages.

The most useful way to model the action in a gamified system is through activity cycles, a concept that has gained traction in describing social media and social networking services. User actions provoke some other activity, which in turn provokes other user actions. Think of a user tagging a friend in a photo she uploads to Facebook, the upload triggering a notification message to the second user, the second user posting a comment on the photo, a new notification going back to the first user, and so on.

There are two kinds of cycles to develop: engagement loops and progression stairs. Engagement loops describe, at a micro level, what your players do, why they do it, and what the system does in response. Progression stairs give a macro perspective on the player's journey.

Engagement Loops

Player actions result from motivation and in turn produce feedback in the form of responses from the system, like awarding points. That feedback in turn motivates the user to take further actions (figure 5.2). The key element here is feedback. Feedback is part of what makes games so effective as motivators. Actions immediately produce visible responses. You know exactly where you stand, and when you do something good, you know it.

Virtually all the game components can be seen as forms of feedback. Points, for example, are a way of displaying feedback about performance, as are leaderboards, levels, and achievements. Thinking in

Figure 5.2: Activity Cycle

terms of feedback keeps you from overemphasizing the specific components or their reward aspects. A reward, after all, is just a kind of feedback. The feedback is what creates the motivation for further actions.

The engagement loop is the basic process of your gamified system. However, it doesn't capture the ways that players advance. Game design consultant Amy Jo Kim points out that gamification experts often come from the world of social media, where quick, temporary relationships are the norm, rather than from the games community, where deep, sustained engagement is the goal. They, therefore, have a blind spot in recognizing the importance of the player journey. If the experience is exactly the same on Day 100 as it is on Day 1, most players will get bored. That's where progression stairs come in.

Progression Stairs

Progression stairs reflect the fact that the game experience changes as players move through it. That usually means an escalating level of challenges. In a game such as World of Warcraft, moving from Level 1 to Level 2 takes far less time and fewer experience points than moving from Level 20 to Level 21 and, in turn, from Level 84 to Level 85. In a gamified system, that equivalent might be the spacing between reward tiers. Map out the player journey in your gamified system as a collection of short-term missions and long-term goals, which play out as a rolling series of progressions.

Though escalating difficulty is the overall tenor of progression, the process shouldn't be completely linear. That's where the progression stairs come in (figure 5.3). The very first stair—often called onboarding—needs to be so simple and guided that it draws players into the game. Once the player is over that hurdle, difficulty ideally should increase at variable rates, along what are called interest curves.

The model used in most games involves steadily increasing difficulty, followed by a period of relative ease, followed by a major challenge at the end of each segment. The rest period allows players to catch their breath. It also lets them experience the satisfaction of mastery: the feeling that they've become an expert at some part of the

Figure 5.3: Progression Stairs

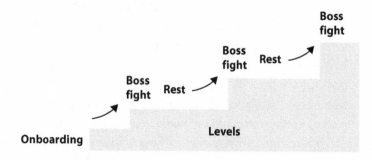

game. There are often a series of small cycles of this sort. The final challenge of a level, known in games as the boss fight, provides for a different experience of mastery. The greatest challenges, which players can just barely surmount, are the ones that produce the explosion of positive emotions that in game terms is called an epic win.

In a gamified system, of course, there probably won't be a "boss" villain waiting at the end of the line. The equivalent is a major challenge that taxes players sufficiently to feel a sense of pride when they reach the next plateau.

Don't neglect to incorporate some measure of randomness. As we noted at Level 4, people like surprises. Studies show that our brains prefer a small, random chance of a big reward to the certainty of a modest reward that over time averages out to a higher number. One need only look at the popularity of slot machines to confirm this finding. Surprises, even small positive surprises, are the way to escape from what is known as the hedonic treadmill: the tendency to take each advance for granted and demand bigger and bigger rewards to stave off boredom. Games do this by sometimes giving you a totally unexpected bonus, or by having one treasure chest out of 10, say, stuffed with far more gold than the others.

5. Don't Forget the Fun!

The last thing to do before you start implementing a gamified system is to take a step back and ask a simple question: Is it fun?

In piecing together game elements and attending to the complexities of players, goals, rules, and motivation, it's easy to lose sight of the fun aspect. We see this often with our students in their gamification projects: They get too wrapped up in the details. Gamification done right is serious business, after all. Yet fun should never be far from your mind. If users perceive the gamified system as fun, they are likely to come back. It behooves you to constantly assess the aesthetic appeal of your system and consider whether it's fun to play.

Ask yourself the following question: Would players participate in your system voluntarily? If there weren't any extrinsic rewards offered, would they still be likely to play? If the answer is no, then you should think about what might make your system more fun.

There are many dimensions to fun. Nicole Lazzaro, a game designer and consultant who is an expert on the emotional aspects of games, found four distinct kinds of fun in studying a group of game players. "Hard fun" is a challenge or puzzle, which is fun because of the pleasure of overcoming it. "Easy fun" is casual enjoyment, a way of blowing off steam without overly taxing yourself. The third category, which Lazzaro calls "altered states," we'll call experimental fun. It's the enjoyment of trying out new personas and new experiences. Finally, what Lazzaro calls "the people factor" is essentially social fun: the kind of fun that depends on interaction with others, even if competitive. Other game designers, notably Marc LeBlanc, offer their own descriptions of the dimensions of fun, involving features like games as make-believe or games as a means of discovering new territory.

The kinds of fun your gamified system should provide will depend on the context. As with player types, don't assume that everyone will want the same type of fun or that participants won't change. The best games offer a broad spectrum of fun. Maybe you're normally attracted to hard-core challenges, but today you just want to blow off steam with your friends. Ideally, a gamified system should be flexible in the same way.

How do you know, though, if a system will actually be fun? For a never-fail answer to that question, you'll need to buy our next book, available for a modest fee . . .

That's a joke. It's intended to make a point: Fun isn't always easy to predict. If it were, game publishers wouldn't spend tens of millions of dollars building games that fail. Fun is an emergent, contingent property that can be fiendishly hard to pin down. The best way to tell whether your system will be fun is to build it and test it and refine it through a rigorous design process.

6.   Deploy the Appropriate Tools for the Job

Finally, we reach the implementation stage. This is where most descriptions of gamification start: picking the appropriate mechanics and components and coding them into your systems. If you've been following us through the levels, you'll see that there is a lot to understand before you start adopting points, badges, and the like. If you've gone through the design steps in this level, you'll be working from a road map rather than merely picking elements out of a hat. You'll know your purpose and your users. The engagement loops you created in the previous step should give you the skeleton of your system. The deployment stage is where you need to pull together the overall experience for your players.

This shouldn't be hard to do in practice, although it's hard to describe the process for every case. As you build your system, you'll see features that emerge from the five Ds that you've already analyzed, and the overall design will become clear. At each stage you'll have to make decisions about what to include and exclude. But that's great. The alternative is to build something shiny and cool and then find yourself wondering why it never actually worked. So you'll need to test, and iterate, and learn as you go. Find people playing games like yours, and ask yourself why they find them engaging. Go back to your project and refine it.

To do gamification well, you'll need a team with a variety of skills. This is not to say that a single person can't implement an effective system—in a start-up, for example—but they will need expertise in more than one area. You will need the following:

- People who understand the business goals of the project; the best game designers in the world may produce something useless if they aren't tethered to the desired strategic objectives
- An understanding of your target group of players and the basics of psychology, which were explained at Level 3
- Game designers, or people who can function like them
- Analytics experts able to make sense of the data your gamified systems generates
- Technologists able to implement your vision

Gamification doesn't require technology any more than games do. However, it lends itself perfectly to online systems. The details of software interfaces and development environments are well beyond the scope of this book, because they change so fast and because there are so many ways to implement a system. Broadly speaking, though, you're going to need a way to track interactions with game elements and integrate those results with your existing business systems.

Some or all of these functions may be delivered by an outside consulting firm or service provider. There are companies that specialize in implementing gamified systems for organizations. The build versus buy decision is similar to others in software and web development. If you choose to go with a service provider, look for one that understands the psychological nuances of gamification. The basic functionality isn't that complicated; the added value from these providers comes from the consulting, customization, and analytics that enable you to optimize your system.

Conclusions (and Beginnings)

If you follow the design process, there is every chance that you will produce an interesting gamification implementation. But there are no guarantees that it will work. Even thoughtful, smart, and experienced developers have to be flexible.

The start-up Lift was incubated by Evan Williams and Biz Stone, founders of the popular social media tool Twitter, and led by Tony Stubblebine, who previously founded CrowdVine, a social networking tool for events. Lift allows users to group around personal goals— losing weight, learning a language, raising money for charity. When Stubblebine and his collaborators first designed and coded Lift, they went through the design process and included a range of established gamification techniques such as we saw in the last level. They thought that this approach would be perfect to encourage users to meet their highest potential. Lift is about helping users track progress to any goal, after all; you would think that adding points and badges would be perfect to motivate users toward their goals.

But they quickly discovered that these elements created all manner of problems: They straightjacketed users into a way of thinking that they didn't like, they were unnecessarily complex, and they caused tracking and programming problems. So Lift jettisoned these elements, went back to the drawing board, and came up with different elements—including a simple "props" button to provide encouragement, and feedback loops based on nothing more complicated than a personal history showing how the user did on a weekly or monthly basis. Eventually, Lift pivoted its business entirely, renaming itself Coach.me and becoming a network for personal coaches. Engagement, it turns out, wasn't its main challenge.

This shouldn't be seen as a failure of gamification or of the design process. Design is an iterative process, and one that is learned by experience. Gamification isn't the solution to every business challenge. The trick is to go out there and practice. Start building gamified processes and see how they work. Playtest the design to see what might work and then see what actually *does* work. Build analytics into your system, change a few things, and see what helps move the needle. Interview your players to see what they liked and didn't like. Go back to the drawing board and start again. There's no shortcut for testing and iteration if you really care about producing a successful gamified system.

Level 6

Epic Fails
And How to Avoid Them

Epic Fail: *Complete and total failure when success should*
have been reasonably easy to attain.
—*The Urban Dictionary*

You've successfully navigated all the basic levels, but there's one more
challenge that can't be ignored. This level is about avoiding traps and
dangers. Here we'll level up by learning what not to do. We'll talk
about the following:

- *Legal and ethical problems*
- *How to avoid the lure of "pointsification"*
- *The dangers of gamification*

In 2011, we hosted the first academic symposium on gamification.
Ian Bogost was the kick-off speaker. Bogost is a noted game designer
and theorist, author of several books (including *Persuasive Games*),
and creator of numerous published games. He's also a leading critic
of gamification.

Bogost's talk was provocatively titled "Gamification Is Bullshit."
He argued that the practice was "invented by consultants as a means
to capture the wild, coveted beast that is video games and to domes-
ticate it." In other words, gamification is all marketing hype that even
the marketers don't believe. Even worse, he claimed, gamification is
employed for purposes that are not in the best interests of players.

Figure 6.1: Cow Clicker

He wasn't just offering a theoretical critique. Earlier, Bogost had created a social game called Cow Clicker, where players clicked endlessly on the image of a cow to accumulate virtual cash (called "mooney"), or paid real money in order to accumulate points and upgrade their cows (figure 6.1). There was no objective other than to satirize gamification. Bogost thought that people would play once or twice, get the point, and move on. Even he was surprised when Cow Clicker went viral and tens of thousands of people became obsessed with their cow clicking—even people who should "know better." A computer science professor topped the leaderboard at one point with more than 100,000 mooney, the result of many hours of clicks.

This is Kathy Sierra's "high-fructose corn syrup of motivation" at work. Cow Clicker is (by design) gamification at its worst: pointless, yet addicting. It's also a warning that serious businesspeople and other practitioners should take to heart.

In this level, we give you a final tier of advice and explain what not to do. Sometimes this will be about how to avoid making ineffective systems, but we're also going to warn you about making gamification systems that are *too* effective. If gamification overemphasizes points and reward systems, as in Cow Clicker, it can replace the richness of games with shallow interactions that are ultimately self-defeating. Also, we'll talk about how to avoid legal and regulatory problems. Then we'll discuss how, if you're not truly acting in the interests of your players, your system can raise ethical concerns. Finally, what happens when your players turn the tables on you and game your game?

Pointsification

The easiest way to miss the potential of gamification is to focus too heavily on the rewards and not enough on the appeal of the experience. This problem can be seen in the unthinking assumption that any business process can be gamified and improved simply by adding points to it and motivating users to engage with the system just for the love of collecting points. Hence the name for the criticism: pointsification.

As you learned at Level 4, there's nothing wrong with using points, badges, and leaderboards, or PBLs, in gamification. There's nothing especially right about it, either. Those three elements are the most common components of gamification implementations, to the point where many people think that PBLs are all that gamification is. If the description of your gamified system starts and ends with these three items, chances are you haven't thought it through.

British game developer Margaret Robertson put it well in a much-discussed June 2010 post on her blog, *Hide&Seek*:

> What we're currently terming gamification is in fact the process of taking the thing that is least essential to games and representing it as the core of the experience. Points and badges have no closer a relationship to games than they do to websites and fitness apps and loyalty cards. . . . They are the least important bit of a game, the bit that has the least to do with all of the rich cognitive, emotional and social drivers which gamifiers are intending to connect with.

Pointsification creates challenges that may require time and effort, but these aren't inherently interesting. They aren't likely to hold most players' interest for long. A small number of players will enjoy it, just as a small number obsessively played Cow Clicker; but not many will. Adding rewards to the points can make the engagement more enduring, but as long as the rewards themselves are the motivating goal, they will be extrinsic motivators. We showed at Level 3 how limited and even counterproductive that approach can be. You can have extrinsic rewards in your gamified system, but understand what those rewards can and can't do. Always look for ways to replace them with intrinsically enjoyable experiences.

Recall that many early gamification examples were glorified loyalty programs. The loyalty industry is largely ignorant of the potential of fun. Think about your frequent-flier program for a minute. Does it feel game-like at all? Is there any social aspect of the process? Any competitive or cooperative game dynamic? Most loyalty programs are about extrinsic rewards—nothing more, nothing less. They aren't designed to be enjoyable in and of themselves. And the obscurity of the exchange rate for rewards can ultimately be frustrating for users. Hence the massive float of unused loyalty points.

To the extent loyalty programs activate intrinsic motivators, they generally focus on status. United Airlines' 1K fliers and owners of the American Express Black Card get special perks for their exalted loyalty program status, but the real benefit is the exalted status itself. For customers who place high importance on status, that's a big deal. Status as a motivator is self-limiting, however, because it doesn't work on everybody, and it taps out when too many people can reach the high echelons. And at the end of the day, if the actual value delivered isn't sufficient, status will be a cold comfort. High-tier frequent-flier members will no longer get excited about "automatic upgrades" when they realize first class is always sold out.

To take advantage of the full potential of gamification, loyalty programs should be incorporated into more comprehensive designs. Jazzing up rewards with badges and leaderboards isn't enough. Today's consumers have seen so many point systems that they are more likely to be weary than amused when they come across another one. The way to avoid this fate is to create challenges that players find intrinsically motivating. Imagine a loyalty program that allowed you to go on quests: Collect miles from flights to three different countries and receive bonus miles or a token of achievement. Imagine one that allowed you to work toward a challenge with family members, friends, or colleagues and that was linked to a social media site that allowed you to coordinate your activities and brag about what you were doing. Or one that placed you on a team to compete against others to amass points for your favorite charity. And so on.

Of course, there are good reasons why frequent-flier programs are only about points. They are cheap and easy, and the executives involved may not want to encourage more engagement with their programs. (Although now that we put it that way, it does seem odd that loyalty programs are so flat and uninteresting, doesn't it?) We're not criticizing loyalty programs. We want to show that even something as points-based as a loyalty program doesn't have to fall into the trap of pointsification.

Our observation here reinforces what we've said throughout the book: Don't think of gamification as a cheap marketing trick; think of it as a deep and subtle engagement technique. A substantial percentage of the gamification examples in the wild today are just pointsification. You can do better.

Legal Issues

Another way your gamified system may fail is by running afoul of legal or regulatory limits. You may not have considered this possibility because there is no body of "gamification law" as such in any legal system in the world. Ignoring legal constraints, however, is a serious mistake.

Some legal problems are common for any digital offering, such as the treatment of personal information about your users. A few, though, are unique to gamification. No project will run into all these issues, because they depend heavily on the nature of the implementation.

There is also significant variation in the law depending on where you're implementing the system.

If you think your gamified service might raise legal concerns, talk to a lawyer. We're not just saying that because both of us have law degrees. Legal experts can advise you on the specific considerations for your particular situation. If they do their job properly, they'll help you understand how much risk you're undertaking and how you could mitigate that risk.

Privacy

Digital privacy is one of the most controversial and uncertain areas of the law. In many countries outside the United States, there are comprehensive data protection regimes, such as Europe's General Data Protection Regulation. Businesses generally must receive affirmative opt-in consent before collecting any personally identifiable information, in addition to other restrictions, such as providing the opportunity for users to review and edit information. The United States tends to be more lenient, focusing on disclosure and the opportunity to opt out. But that may be changing. Major controversies involving Facebook, Google, and a rash of massive data breaches have amped up privacy concerns in the United States too.

Your gamified system can collect a great deal of information about players. As we've discussed, every activity can be tracked. That information can be cross-referenced with other data you have, such as the user's prior transaction history, age, and address. Or you might use gamification to incentivize users to fill out a survey that provides more detailed information about themselves. Make sure you can articulate exactly what information you collect from users, why you collect it, and what you do with it. If you're operating in or collecting data from citizens of jurisdictions such as Europe or Canada with more restrictive data privacy rules, you'll need to ensure that your practices comply. There are also heightened requirements in the United States if you're dealing with sensitive categories of information, such as medical or financial data, or data collected about children.

Any designer of a gamified service should produce a privacy policy for it. Your privacy policy is your representation to your users about what data you will collect, what you'll do with it, and related practices. You're legally obligated to adhere to your privacy policy, although under US law, the policy can be quite permissive. You should keep in mind, however, that public opinion may be more restrictive. Your goal, after all, is for your users to enjoy your service, not to anger them. Sometimes the court of public opinion is the strongest court of all.

Finally, good data protection practices also include data security. The last thing you want is for personal data to leak or be stolen, outraging your users.

Intellectual Property

Intellectual property is the body of law granting exclusive legal rights for intellectual assets. Your gamified system may well involve all four major forms of intellectual property: copyright, trademarks, patents, and trade secrets. You'll want to make sure you're taking sufficient steps to protect any unique assets you're creating. Sometimes this will involve expense, such as filing a patent application for your gamified invention. In the case of copyright and trade secrets, and to a lesser extent trademark, protection will usually happen automatically through your commercial activity and normal business practices.

From a defensive standpoint, take care not to infringe on the intellectual property of others. In most cases that will be easy to avoid. For example, if you like the badge designs on another gamified site, you can't simply copy them and use them yourself, unless the creator authorizes it. The area that is likely to involve the greatest legal risk here is patents. There have been a number of cases in which holders of questionable patents were able to recoup substantial damages from companies that independently developed similar ideas. Gamification is too new to be the subject of significant patent battles, but it's only a matter of time. A study published in 2017 found 134 gamification patents already. Did you know, for example, that the German business software behemoth SAP has patented a design for "Gamification for Enterprise Architectures"?

Property Rights in Virtual Assets

If the assets in your gamified system are valuable in some way, who owns them? You? Or the players who accumulate them? This question is separate from the intellectual property considerations about your creative activities. If users owned their points or achievement titles, they would have rights. They might be able to resell them or prohibit you from, for example, deciding that henceforth it will take 10,000 points instead of 5,000 to reach the "guru" level.

This issue emerged with virtual worlds such as Second Life, which allowed its users to create virtual assets like buildings and clothing. Generally, courts have found that such assets are merely contractual licenses from the game developers, which do not confer property rights on the users. Be sure your terms of service are clear on this point.

Sweepstakes and Gambling

There are laws in many jurisdictions regulating sweepstakes, gambling, and related activities. These come into play when you are offering prizes of some appreciable monetary value. Depending on the circumstances, your gamified service might be considered a sweepstakes, a lottery, gambling, or a contest. All are significantly regulated but in different ways. If the rewards you're offering are of no actual value, such as a badge or an achievement within the game itself, these rules don't come into play. Similarly, if you're offering your own service or a charitable donation, the sweepstakes rules usually don't apply.

Deceptive Practices

If your business model is based on fooling users, you're going to run into the various legal rules prohibiting business fraud. This is as true if you're giving out virtual badges as it is if you're selling stock. The question of deceptive practices can be more complicated for gamification, though, because of the psychological aspects of motivation. What if players are engaged in something because it's fun, but your company financially benefits from their actions?

The basic rule is that users should not be deceived. If they are aware that Procter & Gamble is providing the gamified system as a promotion for one of its products, there's nothing wrong with the fact that they are voluntarily providing marketing benefits for the company. Furthermore, users should not be made to do something against their interest. For example, a gamified system that leads users to choose higher credit card interest rates solely to receive nonfinancial virtual rewards would be problematic.

Advertising

If the gamified system functions as advertising, there are rules about what actions are going to cause problems. These include a baseline prohibition on deception, similar to the previous topic. Beyond that, though, the specifics vary a great deal among jurisdictions. As with privacy law, the United States is significantly more lenient than the rest of the world.

Labor

Generally, businesses have more leeway dealing with employees than with consumers, but employers still cannot deliberately deceive employees or force them to act against their own interests. An employee can be required to play a game as part of his or her job, just like any other mandatory job responsibilities. And the employer can generally use performance in a game-like system as a criterion for promotion or firing. This may not be the case in work environments subject to collective bargaining agreements, or in countries such as Germany where work rules must be defined through structured labor-management processes.

Paid Endorsements

In the United States, the Federal Trade Commission has adopted guidelines requiring disclosure of paid endorsements through social media. The rules were designed to deal with personal blogs that hid the fact that their views about products were sponsored by the creators of those products. However, these guidelines are broad enough to cover gamification. For example, if your service gives users points or other rewards for recommending your product to their friends on Twitter or Facebook, you may need to consider some disclosure.

Virtual Currency Regulation

Virtual currencies add a significant new dimension of legal risk because they connect to real money. Real currencies are heavily regulated throughout the world to prevent fraud, money laundering, currency manipulation, theft, and other problems. Certain activities involving currencies can only be undertaken by banks, which are subject to a plethora of regulations and restrictions. Accounting and taxation also come into play. This is not to say that it's impossible to offer a virtual currency. Virtual worlds such as Second Life and online games such as EVE Online have done so successfully, but only with careful attention to the legal considerations. The rise of cryptocurrencies such as bitcoin, which can be integrated into applications to incentivize activity, significantly complicates the legal landscape.

Future Legal Issues

As gamification becomes more common, we expect to see regulators and legislators become more involved. Inevitably, some company will use gamification in a careless or malevolent way, giving rise to a scandal that provokes calls for legal responses. Equally inevitably, some of the proposed responses will be overreactions crafted by people who don't understand gamification. The best you can do is to keep your eyes open for such developments. And most important, make sure the subject of the scandal isn't you.

The final point to make about legal rules is that you should view them as a floor rather than as a ceiling. This is a fast-changing area, so a borderline practice that seems legally permissible today may be prohibited tomorrow. Moreover, compliance with the law isn't always enough to keep you out of trouble. Ethical and reputational considerations extend above and beyond what the law may require. We turn to them next.

Ethical Concerns

Bogost argues that gamification should instead be called "exploitationware," because it exploits people to do things against their interests or beliefs. We wouldn't go that far, but Bogost raises a legitimate concern.

Laundry workers at Disneyland hotels in Anaheim, California, had a different name for the leaderboard system the company installed in 2011: "the electronic whip." Large flat-panel monitors in laundry rooms showed employees how quickly they fulfilled their tasks and how their speed compared with that of coworkers. The system certainly had an effect. Relationships between workers grew increasingly tense as the work environment became more competitive. Some even skipped bathroom breaks to bump up their numbers.

Perhaps this is what Disney intended. Constant quantitative performance monitoring isn't new, for these hotel laundry workers or for many employees in structured, routine jobs. Public leaderboards seem like a logical next step. Whether the efficiency gains of the "electronic whip" exceeded the costs in worker dissatisfaction is a question only Disney can answer; it certainly didn't seem that way from employees' public comments.

The Disney example isn't atypical. Research has shown that leaderboards alone in the workplace are often demotivating, especially for women. In some contexts, such as sales, contests may be so pervasive that the effects are less significant, but they still show up if systems aren't designed carefully. The problem isn't leaderboards per se. The real issue is any motivational techniques that operate through fear rather than fun. Any athlete who's had butterflies before a big game knows that games can bring out unpleasant emotions along with the positive ones.

At one level, this discussion is a microcosm of normal HR considerations. There has been plenty of analysis on the best ways to motivate employees, and there are many different models that one could point to. However, because gamification is a form of motivational design, it puts a finer point on considerations of employee empowerment and enjoyment. You can use gamification, as Disney did, to control employees more tightly and push them more aggressively. But that forgoes all the benefits of intrinsic motivation. In the end it's important to remember that gamification works over the long run by making things more enjoyable rather than more stressful.

Back at Level 2, we explained that games are defined, in part, by voluntariness. If your employer orders you to play Ping-Pong and declares that your salary will be directly proportional to your score, you're not really playing a game. You may go through the same motions as your opponent, who plays by choice, but your experience is very different. If employers force gamification on their workers, it can undermine the motivational benefits of the activity. Two of our colleagues at Wharton, Ethan Mollick and Nancy Rothbard, found in an experimental study that gamification increased workers' positive affect, but only when perceived as voluntary. In any event, when the system is designed well, compulsion shouldn't be necessary. Liveops, the call-center outsourcer we profiled at Level 3, made its gamified tools voluntary for its agents. Eighty percent of them chose to use them, and of those, 95% remained active.

It should also go without saying that gamification shouldn't be implemented deceptively. Imagine you created a game wherein people matched security photos with mugshots, which turned out to be a way of tracking people without their consent. Deceiving people about your purposes, even if they find the game fun, is an ethical breach, and it is likely to cause bigger problems.

The ride-hailing service Uber secretly used a variety of game elements to push drivers to stay on the road longer than they intended, increasing Uber's revenues. For example, drivers would be alerted that they only needed a few more rides to reach a round number for take-home pay. That activated the intrinsic desire for completion, similar to progress bars on many gamified sites. In this case, though, the number was arbitrary, reflecting Uber's desires rather than those of the drivers. Uber's treatment of drivers is one reason it landed on 24/7 Wall Street's list of the most hated companies in the United States. If you need to hide the fact that you're gamifying, you should think twice about proceeding.

Because gamification is a powerful motivator, powerful actors will inevitably employ it. China is implementing a complex system called social credit that integrates government records to track citizens' compliance with legal and social obligations. The information is made available to cities and to private companies such as Alibaba, which can add their own financial or social media data. For Chinese authorities, game-like scoring systems are mechanisms for regularity of legal enforcement and trust.

Critics in the West see the social credit system as a terrifying gamification of authoritarianism. They foresee an all-powerful citizen score that rises when you do what the state wants (drive below the speed limit or give blood) and falls when you don't (criticize China's crackdown in Hong Kong, or have a friend on social media who does). The system doesn't actually work that way, but the fears are understandable.

Gamification is employed for evil in addition to good. Researchers have found that terrorist groups and violent far-right extremists use PBLs on their secret websites to motivate activity and identify the most committed supporters. Why wouldn't they? Admirers of the gunman who killed 51 people and wounded dozens more at two mosques in New Zealand followed the livestream of his rampage like a first-person shooter video game and commented on message boards about his "high score."

Let us be clear: Gamification in the service of hate and violence is a disgusting perversion of the techniques we describe. But just as we don't condemn websites, mobile phones, and streaming video because terrorists employ these technologies, we must separate gamification from those who use it.

There is nonetheless a tendency to fear new techniques and technologies because of how they can be abused. At the beginning of modern advertising practice, we saw a range of critiques about how advertising, especially television advertising, was turning people into zombies. This moral panic culminated in widespread antipathy toward subliminal advertising, which was supposed to be able to persuade you to do things—buy cigarettes, drink Coke—through images and messages of which you weren't even aware. The efficacy of subliminal advertising is now discredited, and regulation prohibits its use in television and movies. Though advertising has its problems, it's subject to a variety of rules and industry standards. It's now a massively important business model, and largely a phenomenon we've gotten used to. Concerns about the manipulative possibilities of gamification are similar.

If they are not dangerous, then why do people still feel uncomfortable when they hear about game elements being used in marketing or enterprise or social impact settings? In part, there is discomfort over the fact that something people enjoy could be used to profit others. We think everyone should be able to exercise free will. Another consideration is the shock of what's new. As the world becomes more familiar with gamification, we'll see that the unethical applications of gamification are the exception rather than the rule. They deserve your attention, but they shouldn't tar the entire practice.

In the end, people will be themselves. And there's only so much that you can do to influence that. This leads to our final cautionary note. Because sometimes users act in ways you don't expect.

Gaming the Game

A system that incorporates intrinsic motivation will produce a sense of autonomy or agency. Your players need to feel that, in some meaningful way, they are in control. By far the best way to inculcate this feeling is to give them control. That, however, creates its own challenges.

Game designer and consultant Nicole Lazzaro of XEODesign gives the example of the toll system for the Bay Bridge in San Francisco. To encourage drivers to avoid rush hour, the toll goes down significantly at night. The problem with this incentive system is that it encourages some users to play it as a game. Some cars approaching the bridge close to the time just before the toll decreases pull off to the shoulder to wait. When enough cars do so suddenly, it creates a dangerous traffic situation that the designers of the dynamic pricing system didn't anticipate.

Users may find it more enjoyable to play a game of their own choosing rather than the one you've laid out for them. Often this takes the form of exploration. Among the most popular pursuits in "open world" video games such as Grand Theft Auto is to go off the roads (literally) and see what you can find. But in any gamified system, you should expect users to test the edges of your system to see what is there.

Sometimes that turns into gaming the system. If the goals are interesting to the players, some will look for solutions that the designers never anticipated. There are often many ways to do so that don't necessarily amount to cheating. One amusing example occurred when the British government decided to use a gamified crowdsourcing approach to christen its new polar exploration vessel. It didn't expect enthusiastic participants to campaign successfully for the winning name: "Boaty McBoatface."

Gaming the system isn't always a problem. Lloyds TSB Bank implemented an internal market for innovation ideas. It gave its employees a virtual currency, called Beanz, and asked them to submit and rate ideas. The highest-ranked ideas were placed into a virtual stock market, allowing employees to "buy" and "sell" using their Beanz. The Beanz could be cashed out for real money.

The Lloyds system worked exactly as designed—except that users acted in unanticipated ways. First, the virtual economy took off, to the point where hyperinflation was so serious that the supply of Beanz was restricted. Then players realized there was a way to improve their performance on the virtual stock market: insider trading. By affiliating with groups developing ideas, they were able to obtain better information than ordinary "investors" and cash in.

James Gardner, who created the system for Lloyds and went on to develop similar gamified innovation markets at other organizations, says that, initially, his instinct was to stamp out the insider trading. But he quickly realized that this emergent behavior was a feature rather than a bug. The goal of the whole process, after all, was to encourage Lloyds employees to work together more efficiently and develop creative ideas for innovation. In gaming the idea market, employees were doing just that. Working together with the top innovators was the best way to win the game but also the best way to achieve the company's ultimate goals for the project.

The sense of autonomy that users experience when finding unplanned ways to exploit a gamified system can reinforce their intrinsic engagement. You need to be careful, though, because some hacks will crash the game, as the hyperinflation of Beanz demonstrated. It's also a problem if some players gain an unjustified advantage over others, even if they aren't technically cheating. Our recommendations are the ones we gave you in the previous chapter: Iterate and playtest to see how real people engage with your system.

If gamification were a simple algorithm in which input A generated output B, it wouldn't produce particularly interesting results. The reason to incorporate elements of play into business situations is that fun has a powerful pull that logic can't match. For all the analytics and technical manifestations, that makes gamification fundamentally human. The most successful practitioners recognize that people just like them, with all their talents and foibles, are on the other side of the screen.

Endgame
In Conclusion

> *I think work is the world's greatest fun.*
> —Thomas Edison

You've made it to the final level. Here we look back on what we've covered, then look forward to the future of gamification.

The Rochester Institute of Technology houses one of America's top-ranked game-design programs. In 2011 professors Elizabeth Lawley, Andy Phelps, and Elouise Oyzon created a project called Just Press Play to gamify their entire student experience. (Both of us were on the advisory board.)

Rather than redesigning their courses, the project team took a hard look at the things that students really need and what improves their learning outcomes. They discovered that students perform better when they know at least one professor to call on for advice; they are happier when they know their way around campus and around town; they do better when they know how to work in teams; and they do *much* better when they are connected with the community of learning within the entire school. Most of these things can't be built into a curriculum; but you can do it with a game.

To encourage students to get to know their professors, the Just Press Play team printed up collectible cards that students receive in person from a professor when they undertake a quest that the professor designates. One professor, David Simkins, hid his collectible cards in his office, and students had to engage him in conversation as they hunted around his books trying to find their prize. They didn't even notice that they were getting to know the professor—they just wanted the card. Various other gamified elements encouraged creativity, teamwork, and even helpfulness toward other students.

Just Press Play shows how you can use a game-like system to motivate behavior that is important but usually ignored. It is hard to teach teamwork within a normal undergraduate class, so we usually don't bother to try. And no class that we're aware of ever assesses a student on whether he or she can find the office of a professor. But these things turn out to be vitally important to learning, and they can be built into a gamified environment. The flexibility of gamification allowed the RIT professors to identify what they wanted their freshmen to do—"Define your business objective" in our six Ds from Level 5—even though it wasn't within the standard curriculum. And then they worked through the other levels that we've discussed and built a gamified system around that objective.

Not all gamification efforts are as compelling—and sometimes excellent gamification can lead to awful outcomes. Consider the tragic news that Alex Kearns, a student at the University of Nebraska, took his life in June 2020 when he mistakenly believed that he had lost over $700,000 trading stocks on the Robinhood app. Robinhood, a mobile investment platform aimed at millennials, has a cheerful interface and a highly gamified approach to encouraging potentially risky investment bets. For example, to climb the (hugely long) waiting list for a much-desired cash management account involves a gamified feedback loop of tapping on the list—up to 1,000 times a day—to advance a spot. Other examples abound: A user who completes a transaction is rewarded by the app with a burst of confetti; the price of the highly volatile bitcoin is rendered in an attractive shade of pink and placed in a prominent location on the app; and wildly swinging penny stocks are given prominence on the front page.

Robinhood was created by fintech entrepreneurs Vlad Tenev and Baiju Bhatt in 2013, and for a number of years more straight-laced financial news outlets criticized it for encouraging risky investment behavior. "I liken it to giving the keys of a sports car to a 12-year old," said one financial planning educator quoted by NBC News, whose story dubbed it "Charles Schwab meet[s] Candy Crush." Yet it attracted $1.2 billion in venture capital from the likes of Sequoia Capital precisely *because* its frictionless, gamified approach to investment helped produce such rapid growth targeting younger investors.

The Robinhood creators never intended any terrible outcomes from their gamification efforts, and their response to the tragedy has been contrite, heartfelt, and anguished. But the tragedy of Alex Kearns's death is a testament to the power of gamification to alter people's behavior, sometimes to their tragic detriment. Robinhood is a lesson in how gamification needs to be used responsibly and thoughtfully, with an eye toward negative outcomes as well as positive ones.

This book has been about trying to extract as many lessons as possible from the gamification state of art, so that your efforts will be counted among the successful—and ethical—few. In this final level, it's worthwhile looking back at the lessons we've learned and casting our gaze forward to see what the future of gamification may look like.

Looking Back

What have you learned during the course of this book?

First, while points, badges, and leaderboards may be important elements of some projects, gamification is more than just drizzling these elements onto a business process like caramel syrup on a sundae. Gamification requires a great deal of thought about the entire design of the system, including understanding the nature of your users, thinking about what you'd like them to do and how best to make them do it, considering the best technology platform to do that, and examining the specific game elements you're going to employ to get them to do things—among many other considerations.

Along the way we've also learned some very specific lessons about how to implement gamification design. We've developed lessons in motivation and behavior modification that work. We've sketched out ways of thinking about your users. We've discussed methods of connecting different game elements, and when you should and should not use them. And we've seen numerous examples of successful and unsuccessful gamification in a range of disciplines—including your own, one hopes.

One of the most important lessons, however, has gone largely unstated. Our view is that businesspeople need to learn from games, but at the same time, game designers need to learn from business experts. Juho Hamari and Vili Lehdonvirta, two Finnish researchers, studied the way popular massively multiplayer online games from around the world handled virtual goods. They found that their practice mirrored established marketing concepts, including segmentation, product differentiation, life-cycle management, and exploitation of cognitive biases. What's interesting is that the game designers weren't getting these ideas by talking to marketers in non-game industries. They were reinventing them in response to the behavior of their players. The same story is playing out in the gamification world.

This is where you, the readers of this book, come in. The most successful new gamification efforts will come from people schooled in "traditional" areas of business, philanthropy, and government who take the lessons from this book and apply them to fields that they understand and know. Gamification may be the next new thing, but its future will depend on linkages to established fields.

Looking Forward

When we published the original edition of *For the Win* in 2012, gamification was bursting on the scene as, in the words of the *Economist*'s review, "the latest management fad." Nearly a decade later, it's no longer a fad: It's an established technique employed everywhere.

In the first edition, we closed with a section called "Looking Forward," making some tentative predictions about the adoption of gamification in the then-coming decade. We talked then about the inevitable march of gamification into marketing and sales and gave some examples of how gamification platforms would make this easy for people in those sectors. We didn't foretell the development of gamification mechanics in customer relationship management systems, but this is now a feature of many of those platforms. We also thought that gamification would be used extensively within the internal processes of many businesses, to align worker behaviors toward the aims of the business. We thought this would mostly happen within HR systems, a prediction that hasn't yet come true across the board. Finally, we thought gamification would become widespread in the public sector, and especially in the philanthropic and charitable arena. This has certainly happened in a way, although not quite as we anticipated.

Nowadays, the emphasis in behavioral design for public good is through "nudging," which we noted as one of the big five gamification trends in the introduction. Nudging relies on psychological principles similar to those of gamification. It has become so popular within governments that there are entire units devoted to the development of behavioral-design nudges that push people to behave unconsciously in certain civically appropriate ways. Think of it as gamification, without the obvious game layer.

Four other trends we noted have arisen since the first edition: the expansion of gamification into areas outside of business; the adoption of game mechanics beyond points, badges, and leaderboards; the growth of "spot gamification" that utilizes just lightweight game thinking to affect motivation and engagement; and the use of gamification as unprincipled manipulation. Of these trends, we correctly anticipated nonbusiness uses, the adoption of non-PBL game mechanics, and the use of gamification for manipulation. So, three out of five trends, a solid B-plus.

This isn't bad. But on reflection, it wasn't rocket science to see how gamification would grow. The future we see now is less about gamification as a new practice and more about the nuances of effectiveness and the context in which game mechanics are delivered. As an analog, think about how no one needs to persuade corporate executives to create a website anymore, or to have a presence on social media, even though entire forests were harvested in the 1990s and 2000s to provide the paper for books on those topics. Yet we still have a long way to go to employ those digital tools to their fullest potential and navigate their pitfalls. The same is true with gamification: It's clear that gamification will be used more—and in more areas—over the next 10 years than it was used in its first 10. Gamification is almost a teenager now, and it's growing up fast.

Unlike last time, we won't make many specific predictions. But there is one big trend we're prepared to bet on happening. We think gamification will be paired with sophisticated digital A/B testing to segment users and deliver more tailored game-like experiences that appeal specifically to the individual. As we noted at Level 3, certain game mechanics are strong motivators for some users, but are equally strong *demotivators* for other user types. Competition and leaderboards are examples of this: Studies show salespeople, and men, often respond really well to these mechanics, while some other users dislike them. The rise of big data segmentation methods and A/B testing will mean more narrowly tailored game mechanics, designed specifically for what you like. Just as social media means users see only the sort of content they like, in time, users will interact only with the sorts of game mechanics that push their buttons. This will give rise to even more ethical questions than the ones we've discussed.

We hope you have found this book as interesting to read as we've found it to write. Whether you're reading this book to develop a gamification project, because you're curious about a new business practice, because you love games, or for some other reason, we trust that we've given you some ideas to think about, some ways to approach your problem, and some tools to apply.

Good luck in bringing more fun and games into your work. And your life!

Acknowledgments

This book would not have been possible without the support and assistance of many people.

Shelley Kolstad provided invaluable research assistance on the updated edition.

Kevin would like to thank Justin Dunham, Roz Duffy, Karl Ulrich, Ethan Mollick, and Adam Werbach for their contributions to the project. And to Johanna, thanks for being there.

Dan would like to thank Naomi Allen, Stephanie Chichetti, Jill Raines, and Jennifer Williams for their excellent assistance and feedback. And to Shana, because, of course.

We both express our sincere gratitude to Philip Beauregard, Adam Bosworth, Sebastian Deterding, Caryn Effron, David Johnson, Amy Jo Kim, Liz Lawley, Greg Lastowka, Nicole Lazzaro, Thomas Malaby, Andy Phelps, J. P. Rangaswami, Jesse Redniss, Ross Smith, Kurt Squire, Susan Hunt Stevens, and Tony Stubblebine for thoughtful comments on the manuscript or insights in conversation. Steve Kobrin, Shannon Berning, and Brett LoGiurato of Wharton School Press provided excellent editorial support and an opportunity to explore an innovative new form of publishing. The members of the Terror Nova World of Warcraft guild showed us just how much fun games can be (not only when we wrote the first edition and were playing the original WoW, but also now in the time of pandemic, which inevitably drew us both back to WoW, this time in its Classic iteration). The participants in our 2011 For the Win symposium and 2015 Gameful Approaches to Motivation and Engagement workshop proved that even the experts are still making sense of this emerging field. And our students, starting with our inaugural gamification course at Wharton, were the best teachers we could possibly have.

Glossary

Advergames. Games built to promote products or services. Commonly used to increase activity or brand engagement on consumer-facing websites.

Avatar. A virtual representation of a player's character in a game. Common in role-playing games in which the player may take on the role of a magical creature or a medieval warrior.

Badge. A visual token of an achievement. Usually designed to look like the real-world analogs, such as Boy Scout badges or the Good Housekeeping Seal.

Boss fight. A difficult fight against a high-level opponent, called a boss. Often marks the end of a level or a section of a game.

Daily/monthly active users (DAUs/MAUs). The number of individuals who visit your website on an average day or during the course of a month. Common metrics for social games. The ratio of these numbers indicates the intensity of user activity; a DAU/MAU ratio of 50% would mean that half the users visit every day.

Engagement loop. The basic cycle of activity in a game, from motivation to activity to feedback, which in turn motivates further actions.

Epic fail. A major screw-up in a game, such as dying quickly in combat or falling off a ledge by accident.

Epic win. A glorious victory in a game, usually stretching players to the limits of their abilities. Often connected to a boss fight or finishing a game.

Extrinsic motivation. Doing something for a reason other than for its own sake. This could be money, status, power, some other reward you value, direction by your boss, or benefits for someone you care about.

Game. A voluntary activity that operates within a "magic circle," in which players follow the rules of the game rather than those of the real world.

Game component. A particular structure in a game that implements the game's mechanics and dynamics. Points and badges are examples of game components.

Game design. The overall process of creating engaging games, based on an understanding of player desires, technological feasibility, and business objectives. Distinguished from the narrower term "game development," which is the technical implementation of a game.

Game dynamics. The conceptual structures underlying a game, such as the narrative and rules (constraints) that shape the game. These are the most abstract game elements. Players feel their effects but do not engage with them directly.

Game element. A design pattern that can be incorporated into a game. Game elements are the pieces that a game designer assembles in creating an engaging experience.

Game mechanics. The processes that drive forward the action in a game, such as feedback or turns. Game mechanics are the actions that implement higher-level game dynamics and manifest themselves in lower-level game components.

Game thinking. The process of addressing problems like a game designer, by looking at how to motivate players and create engaging, fun experiences. Sometimes called "gameful thinking," in contrast to unstructured "playful thinking."

Games for change. Serious games created for some social benefit, ranging from improving health and wellness to educating kids about the US political process.

Gamification. The use of game elements and game thinking in non-game contexts.

Interest curve. The pattern of gradually increasing difficulty in a game, structured to keep users interested at every stage. Typically, initial levels are easy and quick, to get players hooked, while endgame levels are difficult and long in order to provide sufficient challenges for experienced players.

Intrinsic motivation. Doing something for its own sake. People are intrinsically motivated if they engage in activity without any hope of an external reward. According to Self-Determination Theory, such activities evoke feelings of competence, autonomy, and relatedness.

Leaderboard. A ranked list of participants in a game, with the highest scores on top.

Loyalty program. A program to reward regular customers with benefits in proportion to their levels of activity. Airline frequent-flier programs are the classic example.

Magic circle. The virtual or physical space where the rules of the game hold sway over those of the real world. The concept was introduced by early twentieth-century Dutch philosopher Johan Huizinga.

Massively multiplayer online game (MMOG). Games such as World of Warcraft, in which thousands or even millions of players interact in the same online virtual world. Many such games involve role playing in fantasy or science fiction settings and are sometimes called massively multiplayer online role-playing games (MMORPGs).

Operant conditioning. A theory and process developed by psychologist B. F. Skinner in which behavior is modified by rewards (and, in some approaches, by punishment also).

Play. An essentially unconstrained experience of spontaneous fun, contrasted with the structured rule-based systems of games.

Playtesting. Trying out a game with actual players as a way of garnering feedback. Playtesting can occur with rough versions of a game or even through the use of paper descriptions of gameplay.

Progression stairs. The cycle of advancement through the levels or other steps in a game. Essentially, a more detailed version of the game's interest curve, in which challenges are often followed by rest or consolidation periods along a generally upward trajectory.

Quest. A specific mission or challenge for players of a game. The quest will usually have a narrative and an objective ("collect six Delicious Toadstools from the cave guarded by the Old Troll") and a reward for completion.

Self-Determination Theory. A psychological theory developed by Edward Deci and Richard Ryan of the University of Rochester, along with many collaborators, which defines and emphasizes the importance of intrinsic motivation.

Serious games. Games created for a purpose other than enjoyment, typically some form of knowledge or skill development.

Social games. Online games delivered through social networks, often with a significant element of social interaction.

Social graph. The network of relationships among friends, such as the matrix of connections on Facebook or other social networking sites.

Variable reward schedule. A prize or reward delivered on some nonpredictable basis, such as the payoff of a slot machine. Contrasted with fixed interval rewards (guaranteed at regular time periods) or fixed-ratio rewards (guaranteed for a certain amount of activity).

Virtual currency. A medium of exchange in a game, allowing players to purchase virtual goods or other benefits.

Virtual economy. A functional market system in a game, typically including virtual currency and virtual goods that are subject at least in part to economic forces.

Virtual goods. Virtual items that have value or uniqueness within a game environment. Players may be able to purchase virtual goods with virtual currency, real money, or through achievements within the game. Also called virtual assets.

Virtual world. A persistent online community that allows for virtual interactions between players. Typically, virtual worlds involve immersive 3-D environments, although this is not essential. Most are online role-playing games, but some virtual worlds, such as Second Life, have no gameplay objectives.

Win state. The outcomes of a game that constitute "winning." Typically defined by the rules of the game and the game's feedback or rewards mechanisms.

World of Warcraft. The most successful massively multiplayer online game, a fantasy role-playing world introduced in 2005 by Activision Blizzard. Also known as WoW, it peaked at 12 million paying users worldwide. It has recently been split into two different flavors, with the Classic version played by the cognoscenti and Retail played by N00bs.

Additional Resources

If you are looking to go beyond this book, our website, www.gamify forthewin.com, has additional information on gamification and related concepts. Kevin's massively open online course is at www .coursera.org/learn/gamification.

Here are some references that you may find valuable, including papers we refer to in the book. These works are not all about gamification per se; they expand on relevant concepts that we introduce in this book.

Antin, Judd, and Elizabeth Churchill. "Badges in Social Media: A Social Psychological Perspective." Proceedings of the ACM CHI Conference on Human Factors in Computing Systems, Vancouver BC, Canada, May 7, 2011.

Barankay, Iwan. "Rank Incentives: Evidence from a Randomized Workplace Experiment." 2012.

Bogost, Ian. *Persuasive Games: The Expressive Power of Videogames*. Cambridge, MA: MIT Press, 2007.

Buckley, Patrick, Seamus Noonan, Conor Geary, Thomas Mackessy, and Eoghan Nagle. "An Empirical Study of Gamification Frameworks." *Journal of Organizational and End User Computing* 31, no. 1 (January–March 2019): 22–38.

Castronova, Edward. *Synthetic Worlds: The Business and Culture of Online Games*. Chicago: University of Chicago Press, 2005.

Deterding, Sebastian, Dan Dixon, Rilla Khaled, and Lennart Nacke. "From Game Design Elements to Gamefulness: Defining Gamification." Proceedings of the 15th International Academic MindTrek Conference: Envisioning Future Media Environments, Tampere, Finland, September 2011.

Edery, David, and Ethan Mollick. *Changing the Game: How Video Games Are Transforming the Future of Business*. Upper Saddle River, NJ: FT Press, 2009.

Gee, James Paul. *What Video Games Have to Teach Us About Learning and Literacy*. New York: Palgrave Macmillan, 2003.

Höflinger, Patrick. "Gamification in Proprietary Innovation: Identifying a Technical Framework Based on Patent Data." Proceedings of the 50th Hawaii International Conference on System Sciences, Hawaii, USA, January 4–7, 2017.

Johnson, Daniel, Sebastian Deterding, Kerri-Ann Kuhn, Aleksandra Staneva, Stoyan Stoyanov, and Leanne Hides. "Gamification for Health and Wellbeing: A Systematic Review of the Literature." *Internet Interventions* 6 (November 2016): 89–106.

Jung, Hee-Tae, Hwan Kim, Jugyeong Jeong, Bomin Jeon, Taekeong Ryu, and Yangsoo Kim. "Feasibility of Using the RAPAEL Smart Glove in Upper Limb Physical Therapy for Patients after Stroke: A Randomized Controlled Trial." 39th Annual International Conference of the IEEE Engineering in Medicine and Biology Society, Jeju Island, South Korea, July 11–15, 2017.

Koivisto, Jonna, and Juho Hamari. "The Rise of Motivational Information Systems: A Review of Gamification Research." *International Journal of Management* 45 (2019): 191–210.

Koster, Raph. *A Theory of Fun for Game Design*. Scottsdale, AZ: Paraglyph Press, 2005.

Lazzaro, Nicole. "Why We Play Games: Four Keys to More Emotion without Story." 2004. http://www.xeodesign.com/xeodesign_whyweplaygames.pdf.

Majuri, Jenni, Jonna Koivisto, and Juho Hamari. "Gamification of Education and Learning: A Review of Empirical Literature." Proceedings of the GamiFIN Conference, Pori, Finland, May 21–23, 2018.

McGonigal, Jane. *Reality Is Broken: Why Games Make Us Better and How They Can Change the World*. New York: Penguin, 2011.

Mekler, Elisa D., Florian Brühlmann, Klaus Opwis, and Alexandre N. Tuch. "Do Points, Levels and Leaderboards Harm Intrinsic Motivation? An Empirical Analysis of Common Gamification Elements." Proceedings of the First International Conference on Gameful Design, Research, and Applications, Toronto, Ontario, Canada, October 2013.

Mollick, Ethan R., and Nancy Rothbard. "Mandatory Fun: Consent, Gamification and the Impact of Games at Work" (working paper). The Wharton School Research Paper Series, University of Pennsylvania (September 30, 2014). https://papers.ssrn.com/sol3/papers.cfm?abstract_id=2277103.

Pink, Daniel. *Drive: The Surprising Truth about What Motivates Us*. New York: Riverhead, 2009.

Reeves, Byron, and J. Leighton Read. *Total Engagement: Using Games and Virtual Worlds to Change the Way People Work and Businesses Compete*. Boston: Harvard Business School Publishing, 2009.

Rigby, Scott, and Richard Ryan. *Glued to Games: How Video Games Draw Us In and Hold Us Spellbound*. Santa Barbara, CA: Praeger, 2011.

Robertson, Margaret. "Can't Play, Won't Play." *Hide&Seek*, October 6, 2010. http://www.hideandseek.net/2010/10/06/cant-play-wont-play/.

Salen, Katie, and Eric Zimmerman. *Rules of Play: Game Design Fundamentals.* Cambridge, MA: MIT Press, 2004.

Schell, Jesse. *The Art of Game Design: A Book of Lenses.* Burlington, MA: Morgan Kaufmann, 2008.

Sheldon, Lee. *The Multiplayer Classroom: Designing Coursework as a Game.* Boston: Cengage Learning, 2012.

Walz, Steffen, and Sebastian Deterding, eds. *The Gameful World.* Cambridge, MA: MIT Press, 2015.

Winkel, David J. "Gamification of Electronic Learning in Radiology Education to Improve Diagnostic Confidence and Reduce Error Rates." *American Journal of Roentgenology* 214 (March 2020): 618–623.

Index

Note: Page numbers in italics indicate figures.

About the Authors

Kevin Werbach is a leading expert on the legal, business, and public policy aspects of the network age. He is a professor of legal studies at The Wharton School, University of Pennsylvania, where he currently leads the Reg@Tech roundtable and the Wharton Cryptogovernance Workshop, and he is the author of *The Blockchain and the New Architecture of Trust* (MIT Press, 2018). He co-led the review of the Federal Communications Commission for the Obama administration's Presidential Transition Team and served as an expert adviser on broadband issues to the FCC and the National Telecommunications and Information Administration. For nine years he organized Supernova, a leading executive technology conference. Werbach was previously the editor of "Release 1.0: Esther Dyson's Monthly Report" and served as counsel for New Technology Policy at the FCC in the Clinton administration, where he helped develop the US government's internet and e-commerce policies. Follow him on Twitter at @kwerb.

Dan Hunter is an international expert in internet and intellectual property law, in artificial intelligence and cognitive science models of law, and in legaltech and legal innovation. He serves as executive dean of the Faculty of Law, Queensland University of Technology (QUT), and was previously the founding dean of Swinburne Law School. He holds a PhD from Cambridge on the nature of legal reasoning, as well as computer science and law degrees from Monash University, and a master of laws by research from the University of Melbourne. He has taught at law and business schools in Australia, England, and the United States. Hunter regularly publishes on artificial intelligence, legal technology, and the theory of intellectual property. His most recent books are *A History of Intellectual Property in 50 Objects* (Cambridge, 2019) and *The Oxford Introductions to U.S. Law: Intellectual Property* (OUP, 2012). He is a fellow of the Australian Academy of Law and a chief investigator in the $71M ARC Centre of Excellence for Automated Decision-Making and Society. He also founded the *Future Law Podcast* (http://thefuturelawpodcast.com), which talks about how law is changing during this time of massive disruption.

About Wharton School Press

Wharton School Press, the book publishing arm of the Wharton School of the University of Pennsylvania, was established to inspire bold, insightful thinking within the global business community.

Wharton School Press publishes a select list of award-winning, best-selling, and thought-leading books that offer trusted business knowledge to help leaders at all levels meet the challenges of today and the opportunities of tomorrow. Led by a spirit of innovation and experimentation, Wharton School Press leverages groundbreaking digital technologies and has pioneered a fast-reading business book format that fits readers' busy lives, allowing them to swiftly emerge with the tools and information needed to make an impact. Wharton School Press books offer guidance and inspiration on a variety of topics, including leadership, management, strategy, innovation, entrepreneurship, finance, marketing, social impact, public policy, and more.

Wharton School Press also operates an online bookstore featuring a curated selection of influential books by Wharton School faculty and Press authors published by a wide range of leading publishers.

To find books that will inspire and empower you to increase your impact and expand your personal and professional horizons, visit *wsp.wharton.upenn.edu.*

About the Wharton School

Founded in 1881 as the world's first collegiate business school, the Wharton School of the University of Pennsylvania is shaping the future of business by incubating ideas, driving insights, and creating leaders who change the world. With a faculty of more than 235 renowned professors, Wharton has 5,000 undergraduate, MBA, executive MBA, and doctoral students. Each year 13,000 professionals from around the world advance their careers through Wharton Executive Education's individual, company-customized, and online programs. More than 99,000 Wharton alumni form a powerful global network of leaders who transform business every day.

www.wharton.upenn.edu